Empower Your Fear

Scott Allan is a bestselling author who has a passion for teaching, building life skills, and inspiring others to take charge of their lives.

Scott's mission is to give people the strategies needed to design the life they want through choice.

He believes successful living is a series of small, consistent actions taken every day to build a thriving lifestyle with intentional purpose.

By taking the necessary steps and eliminating unwanted distractions that keep you stuck, you are free to focus on the essentials.

You can connect with Scott online at:
Blog: www.scottallanauthor.com
Amazon Books: amazon.com/author/scottallan

AF621934

Also by Scott Allan

Up to date book releases can be found by visiting www.scottallansite.com or scottallanbooks on Amazon

The Lifestyle Mastery Series

Drive Your Destiny
The Discipline of Masters
The Master of Achievement

The Empowered Lifestyle Series

Empower Your Thoughts
Empower Your Fear
Empower Your Freedom (Coming Soon)
Empower Your Gift of Gratitude (Coming Soon)
Empower Your Social Influence

The Rejection Free Series

Rejection Reset
Rejection Free
Rejection Rehab (Coming Soon)

Break Your Fear Series

Nothing Scares Me [Previously Titles Do It Scared]
Relaunch Your Life
Undefeated
Fail Big
Lifestyle Mastery Series Boxset: Vol. 1 Books 1-3

Empower Your Fear

Turn Self-Doubt into a Confident Plan of Action

Scott Allan

RUPA

Published by
Rupa Publications India Pvt. Ltd 2022
7/16, Ansari Road, Daryaganj
New Delhi 110002

Sales Centres:
Allahabad Bengaluru Chennai
Hyderabad Jaipur Kathmandu
Kolkata Mumbai

ISBN: 978-93-9054-793-7

First impression 2022

10 9 8 7 6 5 4 3 2 1

Printed in India

To Dad
For showing all of us the most valuable lesson there is:
Never give up.

CONTENTS

"Whatever you do, you need courage. Whatever course you decide upon, there is always someone to tell you that you are wrong. There are always difficulties arising that tempt you to believe your critics are right. To map out a course of action and follow it to an end requires some of the same courage that a soldier needs. Peace has its victories, but it takes brave men and women to win them."

—Ralph Waldo Emerson

INTRODUCTION: I KNOW WHAT SCARES YOU

"Expose yourself to your deepest fear; after that, fear has no power, and the fear of freedom shrinks and vanishes. You are free."

—Jim Morrison

When I was a kid, I had this recurring nightmare for about two years from the time I was six years old.

The dream would always begin the same. I'd be lying in bed and would wake up to a knocking on my window from outside. There was a window overlooking my bed, so when I looked up at night, I could always see the stars.

But when the knocking first started and I looked up at the window, the stars were replaced by an old man's white, emotionless face and deep glowing red eyes just staring down at me.

For the first few times, he just looked at me with a pale, blank expression. When the dreams started, I would just hide under the covers until I woke up, which I could only do if I screamed really loud.

It was the knocking that was the most disturbing. The first time I had the dream, I thought it was real. You know, like a false awakening? This was like that. When you're six, you don't know what's real and not; as kids, we're all afraid of the bogeyman. I met mine at least twice a month when he came knocking at my bedroom window.

With every dream, it escalated. The knocking was louder and the fear I experienced more intense. In the beginning, it was just his face silently staring down at me. After several months, he started to say something, but with the window closed, his lips just moved up and down.

When the knocking started again one night, I closed my eyes and waited for it to end, only this time I could hear his voice, dry and crackling from outside. It said, "I know you're scared. Let me in. Open the window. Let me in."

It was like a bad Stephen King novel.

Let me in.

Not a chance.

Those dreams probably lasted seconds but they might as well have been hours.

I told my parents about the dream, and when I was too scared to sleep alone, I'd stay with them. My mother finally said to me, "You should just let him in. Let the man in." The man was what we called him because he had no other name. He was just a monster with white skin, red eyes, and bad teeth. I couldn't believe my mother was suggesting that I let the monster into my room. That was the most terrifying idea I'd ever heard.

That night, I went to sleep, and I woke up to the banging on the window; to this day, I can still see the dream as if it were last week. I remember closing my eyes and hoping again that it would all go away; but then I remembered my mother's words: *Let it in.*

I had a choice to make: Stay scared or do something.

So, I did. In my dream, I got out of bed and faced the

monster at the window; that blank white face stared back at me with those dark eyes, red and swollen and full of hate. His mouth was moving, and I couldn't hear what he was saying, but I could read those parched lips. They were saying, "Let me in."

I reached up and undid the latch on the window. I opened it and invited the monster into my world.

And the dream ended.

I never had it again after that night. There was no more knocking or a ghostly apparition at the window. Over the years, I've had a lot of other nightmares, but the man at the window was gone.

Forever.

I had conquered one of my biggest childhood fears by letting the fear in.

Stephen King would be proud.

Embracing Your Fear

If you struggle with managing the fear in your life, it's time to let the fear in. By embracing what scares you and empowering your fear in ways that are motivating instead of feeding your helplessness, you can develop the habit of taking direct action toward the fear.

Our instinct is to run from the things that are scary, bury our nightmares, and pretend they don't exist. Like the bogeyman that would appear in my dreams as a child, I would hide under the covers praying for him to go away.

As adults, we're still afraid of the dark, and the situations we deal with in our lives can often be compared to a nightmare: being challenged against our weaknesses; facing rejection; financial hardships; or going through a tough transition.

If fear has been holding you back from moving forward, it's time to come out from under the covers and face those demons. When we gather the courage to do this, we discover that the fear is always at its peak before it is confronted.

Here are **five truths** I've learned about fear:

1. The fear is not as bad as you think.
2. The fear won't go away until you deal with it.
3. You'll always fear something.
4. Everyone else has fear, too.
5. 99% of your fears are illusions.

We all have multiple fears. Regardless of what they are, this book doesn't focus on any one particular fear but will give you an action plan you can implement with confidence. You get to embrace what scares you, like the man at my window, and taking a deep breath, let your fears in so you can deal with them and move forward with your life. When you do, it will empower you to no end.

Avoiding our fears is the #1 reason we stay trapped in old routines, boring jobs, unhealthy relationships, and bad behaviors that grow worse the older we get.

By facing what scares us the most, we're empowered to rise up and become much stronger than we had ever imagined. When we decide exactly what we are going to do to diminish our fears, the fear loses its power over us immediately.

Let the Fear In

Can you imagine what it would be like if you could face each day without having any self-doubt? What could you accomplish and dream of doing if fear didn't stop you from taking action?

What if we could wave a magic stick and remove all fear and self-doubt from our lives right now?

What if there was a way for you to do the things you love without worrying about the results or final outcome ending in disaster? What would you do with your life today if you had no fear of money, looking stupid, asking for something, or changing your bad morning routine?

Fear controls our lives in so many ways. It's always there, isn't it? When you have to make a sudden decision and you're not sure if it's right or wrong? When you hear that your company is laying people off and you think you might be next? When the person of your dreams suddenly shows up one day and tells you it's over, and you're left all alone? When you're facing illness or death? When you're in a position of losing everything you've worked for?

"Fear is the main source of superstition, and one of the main sources of cruelty. To conquer fear is the beginning of wisdom."

—Bertrand Russell

Fear is everywhere. It lives "out there" and it lives inside us. If it has its way, that fear will grow more powerful over time and stick to your thoughts like glue. Once your thoughts have become corrupted by a certain fear, we feed into it repeatedly.

Our fear grows larger than we could possibly imagine until it's dealt with. I know people have lived most of their lives afraid of doing the things they wanted to because the thought of facing what scares them was just too much to handle. They failed by letting the fear win.

When we avoid the situations in life that are painful, by

pretending the fear doesn't exist makes it stronger. I wrote this book to help people embrace their personal power and accomplish what they are destined to do.

The purpose of this book is to give you the tools and resources to fight back, to not give in, and to do the things you've always wanted to do without fear of failing or being held back by scarcity thinking.

In this book, I'll show you how I manage to control my fear and how you can, too. You'll be surprised that it isn't as overwhelming as you think. No matter what issues you may be dealing with in your "dark side", you can take comfort in knowing that millions of people the world over are doing things every day that once scared the pants off of them.

For many, there's a lot of shame in being afraid. We think that being afraid of the dark is for kids. But the truth is that we're all still afraid of the dark, aren't we? Only the darkness has become our lives and the monsters are all the people and institutions in control of our lives. We're afraid of living and that has become the worse fear of all.

You might have experienced fear in these areas:

- The first day at a new job
- Looking for a new job/going on job interviews
- Being employed in a job you hate and wanting out
- Facing responsibility for something you did
- Making hardline choices
- Retiring alone
- Raising your kids
- Losing people that you love
- Taking charge of your financial future
- Looking at the clutter in your house and feeling overwhelmed

- Feeling helpless when your child has a problem
- Being alone for the first time in your life
- Wanting to get out of a relationship but feeling trapped
- Visiting the hospital because of a health issue
- Being asked to do something you've never had any experience with
- Giving a speech or presentation in front of 200 people

The mistake many people make when dealing with fear is that we look for ways to brush it under the carpet. Out of sight; out of mind. Let's be honest; facing our fears is difficult. If we could, wouldn't it be better just to wish them away, so we never have to deal with any of it?

For many years, this is how I dealt with many of my issues. I would put them off or get purposely distracted doing something else, so I didn't have to think about anything. It works temporarily, but in the long-term, the stuff you don't deal with eventually deals with *you* in its own way.

Empower Your Fear focuses on real solutions you can apply for long-term results that stick. This book will teach you to develop deeper strategies for empowering the fear when it's keeping you trapped. You'll learn to leverage the strength and drive you have to funnel your thoughts and energy into doing simple tasks that chip away at your fear-based mindset.

Most people associate their fears with self-identity. If I'm scared, I must be a coward or weak. This isn't the case. We simply have not developed the skills to deal with many of life's situations. Our fears are learned responses we developed from listening to and observing how others deal with their own fears in life.

You're NOT your fear. You're a fearful person who's been trained to fear what you can't control. You experience fear, but it isn't who you are. You can rise above whatever circumstances are keeping you from reaching and exceeding your greatest potential and achieving your ultimate goals.

Our fears appear larger than life only because our goals and dreams are not. When you make the switch to living an empowered lifestyle, you won't even think about how scared you are. Fear disintegrates when we act with courage.

You have to think of your fear as an ally and companion, and not the monster under the bed that you're trying to get away from. Like the monster that haunted my dreams when I was a kid, all it wanted was for me to let it in.

You can do the same. Let it in and embrace it. When you empower your fear by accepting it and acknowledging it exists, you gain the upper hand and take back control of your life. Instead of feeling physically fatigued and emotionally drained, you become energetic, confident, and assertive.

Your thoughts have incredible power and are the key to diminishing your fears on every level. Learn to master your thoughts about fears, and the battle is half won. The fear you have is yours. Nobody else handed it to you.

Taking responsibility for your situation is the first big step to fear mastery. Once you can recognize and accept that you're creating your fear, there's a shift in the paradigm of how you identify with your fear-based center (more on this later).

You can overcome your limitations that are imposed by fear. You're limited only by fearful beliefs. The level of fear you have is directly related to the amount of self-doubt, worry, anxiety, and a host of negative emotions you pour into it.

The good news is that you don't have to tackle your biggest fear first. You don't have to take on all your fears at once, either. Just choose the one thing that's causing you to stay stuck and start by taking a small action step toward it.

This step could be anything.

You might have to talk to someone about an important issue, and the fear of approaching that person is causing you to procrastinate. It could be something as simple as filling out an application form or creating a checklist of action items for a goal you want to start working on. You might fear that first step, but it's one of the biggest hurdles. Taking one small action will lead to more.

Who is This Book For?

Empower Your Fear focuses on giving you the tactics and confidence to handle fearful situations. By tapping into your power of leverage, eliminating any self-doubt and worry, and taking affirmative action, you can condition yourself to handle anything. There's nothing beyond our scope of repair.

You were dealt the hand you have, and you can play it any way you want. We're responsible for our own lives, and once we realize this, we'll be responsible for our fears, too. Knowing this empowers you to do something about it.

I promise you that by the time you're finished reading this book, you'll be able to convert your fear into fearlessness, self-doubt into confidence, and emotional paralysis into actionable steps. You'll discover that the stuff that scares you is really calling you to take higher action.

Whatever you fear doing is really trying to communicate and encourage you to move forward with your goals and dreams, and to turn emotional paralysis into an action plan. You'll learn tactics to disengage the voices that are keeping you trapped and engage the courage and self-esteem needed to elevate you to make powerful choices with lifechanging results.

Tell Me About Your Fear Monster

In the beginning of this book I told you my story of the monster at my window. Now, what's *your* fear monster? What are you afraid of doing that you haven't faced yet? What scares you more than anything? What makes you feel paralyzed and unable to think?

Some common fears are:

- Change
- Applying for a new job
- Meeting new people and socializing
- Breaking out of a hopeless rut
- Changing a bad habit
- Rejection
- Writing a book/*not* writing a book
- Public speaking/looking stupid in front of a bunch of strangers
- Taking a test/*not* taking a test
- Asking your manager for something, such as a vacation
- Quitting your job (you know, the one you hate going to?)
- Bankruptcy

What would you do right now if you had no fear at all? When I asked myself these questions years ago, I wrote everything down in a journal.

If you haven't developed the habit of keeping a journal to record your thoughts and ideas, I'd suggest making it a daily habit from today. It builds clarity and solidifies your mission.

I found that just by writing out my fears, worries, and pain points, and by bringing these emotions to the surface by writing honestly how I was feeling, I was able to acknowledge them with greater clarity.

Making Your "Fears List"

Here's a simple activity to get warmed up: Make a list of the fears you have. Spend some time on this. Don't worry how silly they may seem. Nobody has to see this list except you. Ask yourself interview questions about each fear: Why am I afraid of this? What would happen if this fear became real? What could happen if I do nothing? What could happen if I do something? Why am I running away from this and avoiding the situation?

Make a list of questions and really drill down to the core truth. This exercise, performed every day, is going to snap your thoughts out of a trance. When we lead fearful lives and avoid the stuff that's uncomfortable, our thoughts shut down on the subject.

Fear avoidance is the #1 reason our fears take over. By questioning your fears, you are bringing those uncomfortable emotions to the surface. From there, you can examine, interview, and take action if you desire.

Most people feel the fear, but that's it. They become overwhelmed. Then their actions become reactions. Their first instinct is to flee, hide, or get busy doing something else. When they question their fears, they lose power. When they can see the "why", the solutions become obvious. Then, they can work on action steps that move them into handling the fear.

Once you know the "why", brainstorm three simple steps you could do to start moving toward the fear. When you move into the fear instead of running from it, you bridge the gap between what you are afraid of doing, and what becomes your greatest victory.

You have to identify what the fear is, why you have it, and then make your "what if?" strategy.

Our fears are only as big as we make them out to be. If you ignore what scares you, the fear will always be there. It will fill you with guilt and paralyze you. You'll criticize yourself for not taking action or having the courage to do anything.

This only makes it worse. Don't beat yourself up for being afraid. *We're all afraid.*

You'll always have fear, too. Whenever you move out of your comfort zone (that is, do something different) the fear is there waiting for you. That's good. Let it push you back. You push back too and climb through to get to the other side. You'll only break your fears if you learn to open that door yourself to see what lies behind it. Nobody can make your life choices. Only you can.

Remember: We're all afraid.

Are you ready to let the fear in?

Are you ready for living a fearless life and empowering your fears to rise above any challenge?

There's no time to waste.

It's time to start living your life and doing what really matters.

Life is meant for living in fulfillment and happiness and not living in fearful states of helplessness.

Now, let's turn the page and get started.

"Of all the liars in the world, sometimes the worst are our own fears."

—Rudyard Kipling

1

MINDSET SHIFT: FEAR-BASED TO POWER-CENTERED

"One of the greatest discoveries a man makes, one of his great surprises, is to find he can do what he was afraid he couldn't do."

—Henry Ford

In this chapter, I'm going to show you two mindsets that describe:

1. How we live in a fearful state, and;
2. How we're empowered by moving into a positive state

These two mindsets are: the **fear-based mindset** and the **power-centered mindset.**

The Fear-Based Mindset

I want you to think of your "mindset center" as being divided in half. One center is where we generate fear. This is the center we tap into right away when a new challenge is suddenly thrown at us. You may have a fear of public speaking, or you just got rejected after your fifth job interview.

When we're fearful and full of negative or fearful emotions, such as doubt, worry, anxiety, helplessness, or depression, our minds are stuck in the fear-based center. People who expend their mental energy in this state of mind are more prone to physical and mental illness, depression, negativity or fear-paralysis.

In this state, they can walk around feeling confused, frightened, and angry with themselves for lacking the know-how to deal with life's problems even at the most basic level. They'll feel paralyzed to do anything about their situation and struggle to come up with a positive solution to their problems.

When we try to live and function in this mindset, it puts us in a place of deep suffering. We have a lot of worry about the future; we thrive in scarcity thinking and believe life's challenges are designed to defeat us.

We may expend tons of energy trying to avoid fearful situations: relationships that hurt, changes we don't want to implement even when it's for the best, or moving toward a new position that requires more responsibility. Whatever the fear is, it begins in this place: The fear-based mindset.

Fear-Based Center Identifiers

- Having an indecisive, excessive obsession with having a failed outcome
- Preferring the comfort of inaction and staying in a rut—even if it causes emotional pain
- Having moments of helplessness and anxiety when faced with life-changing moments
- Being full of self-doubt
- Having a fear of failure and expecting it in most situations

- Focusing on past failures and mistakes; fearing the future because it will bring more painful events
- Imagining the worst possible outcomes
- Making choices based on limited references
- Believing limitations are imposed by external circumstances
- Feeding into distractions to escape problems or challenges
- Staying friends with a "fearful" tribe
- Experiencing feelings of helplessness
- Taking toxins to numb the emotional pain that drives fear
- Having a lot of stress brought on by worry over future events that are not here yet
- Believing the past is the future
- Avoiding risk to avoid getting rejected

Your fear-based center is powerful. You have thoughts, habits, and beliefs that have been shaped and molded to respond to your fearful instincts. The fear model represents the mindset of someone who's living in a fearful state.

As you can see, their choices are limited; they stick to a routine—even if it's a damaging one. They lack confidence and are full of self-doubt. These emotions create a vacuum of fear. The voices of fear keep them trapped in their own hell.

Here are some examples:

- You could be stuck in a job you hate but are too afraid to change.
- You could be in a relationship that sucks but leaving is too painful.
- You could be afraid of rejection, but you're too frightened to go out there and do something about it.
- You could have a fear of forms and paperwork, so your office looks like a disaster zone.

- You could be holding back on giving because you're afraid of losing what you give away.

I know how you feel. Fear is what confined my life to a mediocre state of living. I was fearful in most areas of my life. There's nothing worse than knowing you have great potential to do anything you want and feeling helpless to do anything about it. It's like having the keys to your own magical kingdom and you just can't seem to open the right door.

Power-Centered Mindset

High confidence, self-esteem, positive thinking, and a relaxed state of mind are found in the power-centered mindset. When you're experiencing optimism and that "get out there and do it" attitude, you're trying to achieve, and you can function from a place that's filled with positive energy.

If you can sustain the majority of your time in this area, you're going to be more relaxed, have more energy, and enjoy your life more, knowing you're moving in a clear direction. You're able to make clear choices and bond with the right people to enhance your social interactions. You won't worry about the future; you'll be too busy creating it.

Your power-based center is a life defined by confidence, high self-esteem, goal achievement, taking healthy risks, and taking responsibility for your actions and your life. In this positive based center, life is good and has a clear meaning with a steadfast purpose. We all want to be in this place to succeed, stretch beyond our comfort zones (i.e., mental prisons), and live life to the fullest.

So why is it so hard to get to this place, to stay there, and to stay strong and free of your fear?

Whenever you're in a situation that challenges you to try something new or act in a way that you've never done before, you experience fear. That's good. Having the fear of something is the first step in dealing with it.

How often are you afraid of something that you've done a hundred times? When challenged to step outside yourself, the dynamics change. You trigger emotional anxiety. You'll question your sanity. This creates panic. You stop and ask yourself, "What's going on? This morning, I was so confident and full of high esteem; now I'm shaking in my boots."

For us to gain greater control over our lifestyle choices, we have to face the stuff that's hiding beneath the surface of our fearful lives. All of this is thriving in the fear-based mindset. It is there that we experience the energy of fear.

When we can move away from that fear-based control, and take steps toward the power-based mindset, our thoughts are clearer. We're at peace with ourselves. Anxiety and worry slip away to nothing.

This is your fundamental goal: to thrive in the power-centered mindset that creates your life, defines your goals, and builds confidence. People who are focused in this area are better equipped to deal with problems and create effective solutions. You will feel better and more relaxed, and you will look at the positive side of living.

The fear-based center plays an important role. It's like the warning bell when disaster is approaching. If you're having fearful thoughts and you choose to ignore this, you push that fear down so it doesn't exist in your mind. The problem with this is that now it operates subconsciously at the bottom of your fear-based center.

Power-Centered Identifiers

- Empowering fear through conscious observation and taking action
- Feeling more confident to handle anything that comes along
- Feeling driven to do something out of the fear of not succeeding and leveraging fear to succeed
- Giving without expectation
- Building tribes of fearless warriors
- Pushing to rise above mediocrity
- Overcoming resistance and working on action tasks to avoid distractions
- Having clearly defined goals and setting up daily mini goals to work toward them
- Living in the present moment and making decisions focused on building a powerful destiny
- Focusing on building confidence
- Believing in success—even after failure or when times are tough (power-based people stick to it!)

This book is focused on two primary objectives:

1. Moving you out of a place of defeat, which is your fear-based center. When we operate in this mindset, our focus creates worried thoughts, excessive tension, and stress.
2. Increasing your presence within your power-based center, which is the station where you build confidence and self-esteem. Our presence within this station is focused on personal empowerment and building mental strength

When you're living in your fear-based center, you're stuck. You feel congested and lacking confidence. In the power-based center, you're alert, confident, and in control. You still might be experiencing fear, but it's manageable. You can change anything your heart desires. It's your present limitations that stop you dead in your tracks.

If you feel trapped by self-doubt, you can change that. If you feel overpowered by challenging situations, you can learn to handle the situation with confidence, no matter what.

When you live your life from a place of fear or a mindset that's focused on fearful actions and outcomes, you create suffering. This results in poverty-based or scarcity-level thinking. You fear change and resist taking action. Your life becomes mediocre, not because you're mediocre but, because your ability to confront your fears and leverage them to work for you defines your level of joy, satisfaction, and success.

Successful people have just as much fear as anybody else; the defining difference is that they push forward and break their resistance to change. They define their lives by the actions they take despite the difficulties. They challenge mediocre ideas and struggle forward to rise to the next plateau. They know what they have to do to get where they desire to be—no matter what stands in their way.

Regardless of your financial situation or the place where you were born and raised, you can rise above your limitations. You don't have to settle for what the world gives you. That's a big mistake in believing that you'll never be more than what society gives you.

Everyone starts off someplace different. Some people are born in poverty; others are born in mansions of gold. It's what you *do* with the pieces you're given that determine your fate.

Some people have higher to rise than others. But it's not the length of the reach that matters; it's how far you're willing to reach for your freedom. If you give up, you'll never know how close you were to making it.

Viktor Frankl lived in the worst conditions imaginable from 1942-1945. A holocaust survivor and trained psychiatrist, he spent three years surrounded by death, murder, suicide, and atrocities that nobody could even fathom.

During his imprisonment, Viktor watched thousands of men and women perish. Many died because they lost hope. They gave up and could see nothing to live for. Viktor came to realize that you couldn't always control the circumstances thrust upon you, but you could decide your attitude toward it. It's the only thing you can change.

In the camps, Viktor Frankl observed:

> *"Instead of taking the camp's difficulties as a test of their inner strength, they did not take their life seriously and despised it as something of no consequence. They preferred to close their eyes and to live in the past. Life for such people became meaningless."*

Viktor Frankl clearly demonstrated that he made a clear and conscious decision to move his thoughts from a fear-based mindset to a power-based center. His ability to do this for his own survival is what kept him alive until the end of the war. Many of his companions fell victim to helplessness and fatigue. They gave up or were too weak to carry on, and they perished.

You can apply this power to your own life. You can resign yourself to your present condition as something beyond your control, or you can stay in the present moment and do what it takes right now to change things.

You can never change anything in the past: failures, loss, or misfortune. Your past is not your future, but if you choose to live there, if you focus on doing the same things repeatedly and expecting a different outcome, your future can become your past.

Throughout this book, I'll refer to both of these mindsets, and we'll cover the strategies needed to move from one mindset to the other. It will take diligent practice, but with a determined effort, you'll be more focused and able to recognize when you're suffering in the fear-based mindset.

2

BREAKING AWAY FROM FEARFUL HABITS

"The only way to overcome your fears is to do the thing you fear."

— Brian Tracy, bestselling author of *Maximum Achievement*

In this chapter, we will look at the six ways in which we let the fear stick. Many times, it's what we *don't do* that contributes to the fatigue, stress, and compulsive worrying that creates fearful thoughts.

If we continue to reinforce the habits, thoughts, and behaviors that exist in our fear-based center, our fear will take control of us both physically and mentally.

The 6 Causes of a Fear-based Lifestyle

1. A lack of planning for the future.

For many years, I had no plan for the future. I didn't have any goals or aspirations. I lived for the moment and just accepted whatever life delivered.

However, while living in the moment may be good advice

on one scale, on the other, it's a formula for inviting anxiety into our lives. When you fail to plan for the future, you're leaving the greater part of your destiny to chance. This causes worry for the future and makes us feel as though we have no control over our lives.

One of the roots of worry is caused by living a life without any real concrete plans. With no sense of direction, you end up living a life doing the things you don't want to do for people you don't want to work for. This is how we become trapped in relationships we resent or by working in dead-end jobs that lead to nowhere.

Putting together a viable plan for your future can significantly reduce your fear of future events. This doesn't have to be a perfect, immaculately detailed plan but spending some time each week reviewing your goals will place you in the power-based center.

Think about the things you worry about: Job security, financial planning, health, family, kids, and retirement. Uncertainty and unknowing creates fear. Worry is a trigger that something should be taken care of. People who have a clear sense of direction experience significantly less worry than those who have no plan at all.

Your life doesn't have to have an exact roadmap, but you have to at least know in what direction you're heading. If not, you'll wake up with this fear every day until you do something about it. A life without any plan is like taking a vacation without a destination.

Take a good look at the areas of your life that cause you to think fearfully. Is it your finances? Your career? Your relationships? Your retirement? Narrow it down to only those things which you can control. Many of your fears are beyond what you can do anything about. You can worry about an earthquake occurring, but you'll be powerless to stop it.

But living in fear of losing your job is a situation you can control. You might not be able to stop your company from kicking you out the door when layoffs happen, but if you put in the time to learn a new skill on the side you'll be prepared if it does happen. This is an example of how we can leverage our fear to plan better.

Identify the fears that you have in the key areas of your life. Ask yourself, "Is there any planning I can do for this?" For example, people who have no plan for their financial future are going to be filled with a level of uncertainty, doubt, and, anxiety.

You might be thinking, "But many people fail to plan for the future. Isn't it okay to just take life as it comes?" So much is left to the whims of chance. One might think, "*What if my plan fails or doesn't work out? Planning is a waste of time because so much of life is unpredictable.*"

There is nothing wrong with living day-to-day, but you will enjoy those days much more if you remove that underlying fear that comes with having no plan at all.

We don't know what the future brings. But I can tell you what it's bringing if you don't plan anything: more fear! You don't know what's going to happen in the financial markets or to your place of employment. But the two hours you set aside for doing a rough financial plan are far better use of your time than the two hours spent tonight watching TV.

Make a rough plan for your future at the very least; watch TV later.

Be aware of your excuses. They'll stop you from moving forward.

Here are four steps you can take right now:

a) Identify your one major goal for this year.
b) Create a simple statement to yourself in the form of an affirmation that sets out your goals for the next six months.
c) Write down the one thing you're most worried about.
d) Create a solution (i.e., action steps) for this worry point.

2. Thinking somebody else will take care of it.

Putting other people in charge of your life is risky. Yes, you need support and a level of care to help you through life's tough spots. However, relying on any one system or person creates fear. Why? If anything happened to your crutch, then you're doomed. Taking responsibility for the certain areas of your life is key to reducing and actually eliminating fearful situations.

One area that most people worry about is having no money. But if you set out to create a simple financial plan for yourself, you can quickly take care of this. You're not good with your money or finances? Most people aren't. They don't learn about financial planning in school. And, in most families, financial planning is rarely discussed. Often, they learn about these things too late after they're in debt. And then they really have cause to worry.

If you rely solely on any one person to take care of your needs, eventually, you're going to be left out to dry if something happens to that person. When you place all that trust in another person and give them the responsibility for taking care of you, you're setting yourself up for a possible future mess.

In one particular case, a woman I once knew left everything

to her husband. He took care of all the bills, signed all the papers, and managed their lives. She felt safe and secure. But when he died of a sudden heart attack, she had no idea where anything was. She couldn't even find the bankbook.

Of course, when you have family, you rely on each other for certain parts of the family function. Everyone has a role to play. In an office or place of employment, you're given a certain level of responsibility. Even if you're not playing a certain role, you can make things easier for yourself by learning as much as possible.

When you try to pass the buck and say, "It isn't my problem," there may come a day when it *will* be your problem. You can reduce your fear by staying in tune and keeping informed.

3. Believing you can't deal with your fear.

There was a time in my life when I believed I couldn't deal with most of the things that happened to me. My thinking that the fear was always bigger than me is what defeated me. I would see problems as huge monoliths that controlled my life.

When you think that your fears are in control, they are. You worry about all the bad stuff that's going to happen but never does. Someone once said, "99% of the stuff that I was afraid of never actually happened."

We fear the unknown because it's unpredictable. What happens if I lose my job? Lose money? Lose my wife and kids? We spend all day wondering about the negative stuff that's waiting just around the corner, playing the "what will I do if" game. I can tell you what you're going to do. You're going to have a plan in place so that you can handle and confront any fear that comes your way.

Will worrying help your situation? Has it *ever* helped? Worry is an emotion that you don't need. It serves no purpose at all. It just drives your confidence down and raises your anxiety. If you suffer from worry, chances are that you're living in fear, and you're stuck in the fear-cycle of helplessness. You have to get off the treadmill of fear creation.

Tell yourself: "I can deal with anything that comes my way."

For example, look at where you are today. Chances are that you've already been through several ordeals in your lifetime. Everyone has had to face something. If you're sitting here reading this book, I can assume that you survived it, right? Take a look at some of the news stories out there.

Check out the situations other people are going through. Imagine yourself in a situation that's beyond you. Could you deal with it if you were permanently injured in a car crash? Could you deal with it if you had no money and were completely bankrupt? Could you deal with it if someone you loved died?

You're stronger than you think. I'll wager anything on it. And that which doesn't kill you makes you a better fighter for the next time around. By facing your fears and empowering yourself by feeling the fright, you condition your senses to handle it.

I look at situations I went through years ago that seemed very terrifying and now they don't seem so bad. Why? Maybe I've grown and can handle more now. There are a lot of things I haven't experienced yet either, and when I think about them, I start to trigger the worry button. I start to think, "*What if...?*" and then the cycle will repeat itself.

Take some time to look back on all the events you've worried about and feared. How many of those fears came true? Did you get through those tough times? Did you handle your fear at the time? The #1 reason we stay stuck is because on a subconscious level, we're convinced that we cannot handle what life throws at us.

Make a list of scenarios you fear and ask yourself, "How can I handle this?" Some examples may include:

- If I get divorced, how can I handle this?
- If I lose my job, how can I handle this?
- If I have no money and end up declaring bankruptcy, how can I handle this?

What I know is that there's nothing new that others haven't handled before. I look at the suffering of people all around and see them handling life's difficulties. They struggle and suffer but they're handling it.

It's okay to suffer through a rough spot but keep your thoughts on getting through it so you can get to that happy spot again. When faced with a fearful situation, visualize how you will feel after you get through it. When you prove to yourself that all your fears are really illusions, they are revealed as lies that have no place in your life.

4. I'll avoid it until it goes away (and it never does).

It's easy to just sweep painful and uncomfortable emotions under the rug. I know. I've done it many times. *I'll deal with it later,* I thought. Only, later turned into months—and eventually years.

Most of the fear that controlled and governed my life could have been handled if I had accepted and confronted the fear right when I first felt it.

But, that's life. Only you don't have to waste years hiding from your fright. There will always be something you're afraid of. There will always be fear as long as you keep trying different things. It's not about "getting rid of your fear" because you can't. But, you can learn to handle it better.

Remember: What you resist, always persists.

What are you avoiding right now? What could you do right now to confront this fear? Is it a relationship problem? Is it something at work? First identify the location of your fear. This narrows it down and improves concentration. You have multiple fears in many areas, so it gets overwhelming.

But imagine if you spend a few minutes each day asking yourself this one powerful question: "What am I avoiding today? And why?" When I put this exercise to the test, I made it a point to identify with the fears I had every moment. I would count the fear moments. I was amazed at what scared me. Just sitting at the computer I'd have those fear moments.

Our fear is like a signal; it warns us that something's wrong. Whenever I find myself putting off something (i.e., fear avoidance) or making excuses for why I can't do something, in most cases, I'm afraid of taking action. When I narrow it down further, I'm afraid of doing something because I might fail or look stupid.

Why am I afraid of failing? Because it will confirm my deeper beliefs that I'm no good, and I'll risk losing something valuable because I took an unnecessary chance.

So, you see, you can walk through the situation and get to the root of the problem. Fear has a reason; if you find it, then it's so much easier to overcome and live a happier, healthier lifestyle. What's the reason you're afraid? Hint: It's most likely something you haven't done or are avoiding.

5. We're afraid to admit that we're afraid.

Our society and culture has lied to you. They told you that fear is a sign of weakness. They were wrong. When I was growing up, I was conditioned that failing is a bad thing. After all, what happens when you fail a test? You get a big red pen mark on your paper and a disapproving look from your teacher and classmates. You FAILED.

The F said it all. So, if you were like me, you tried harder next time. You felt motivated to push past the F and get a D on the next test, and a C on the test after that. Your motivation to *not* fail became your energy. You may not know it, but you have a lot of power within your own mind. You can choose to be afraid and do nothing, or you can take that fear and make it work for you.

You have two choices at the end of the day. Deal with the things that scare you or run from them by seeking distractions to avoid them. Whatever way you choose to deal with it, the fear won't go away. You can bury it under a busy schedule, but the fear won't remove itself. It needs to be leveraged.

When you acknowledge the fear in a situation, it makes it real. You become more focused. You can't waste mental energy worrying about something if you're facing it courageously and willing to do something about it.

You see, fear isn't just a feeling; it's an emotion that's trying to communicate with you. It's telling you, "Hey, something's wrong." The challenge is in recognizing what the fear is trying to communicate to you. Is there something that hasn't been done? Have you been avoiding a task that needs your attention? Is there something that should be planned out?

By tapping into your fear, it goes away—just like that! Half of dealing with fear is recognizing that it exists. Ignore it, and it grows more powerful—just like my nightmare did.

6. We don't want to fail, so we do things that are easy and familiar.

The fear of failure is one of the most devastating fears there are. It affects everything we do, and because it's so ingrained into us from past conditioning, we have adjusted ourselves to avoid experiencing it again and again.

This is most prevalent with the fear of rejection. Do you remember the first time you experienced rejection? It hurt, didn't it? To work around this fear, we engage in and limit ourselves to what we know and what we know we're capable of.

Do you find yourself stuck in the comfort zone doing work that's familiar and low risk? Are you involved in a relationship that sucks but stick with it because it's easier than going out on a limb and getting shot down?

By doing what comes easy, you also accept the consequences. In taking the way that is less challenging in the short term, we are setting ourselves up for a life of hardship in the long term. This is how your fear is encouraged to keep you stuck.

7. We have been taught through conditioning that fear is bad

We watched our peers, parents, and other people deal with fear by engaging in fear-based habits. People overeat or devour junk food to deal with fear and stress.

Addictions and compulsions are signs that fear is working in our lives, but instead of confronting it and challenging the obstacles that stand between us and our dreams, we go the other way—we run! It's like the old expression, "F.E.A.R stands for 'Forget Everything and Run!'" I think we've been running enough.

8. We go to bed with unresolved issues.

Sleep is incredibly powerful. You're not just catching sleep so that you can function the next day and start all over again. You sleep for reasons. One of those core reasons is to process what's happening in your life. Here's why: When you sleep, your body and mind go into rejuvenation mode. They repair themselves and process information rapidly. In many ways, they act like computers that need downtime to back up all the data. You effectively go offline for a short time during this process.

If something is recognized by your mind as "incomplete," you might wake up with that ping of doubt or concern. This turns to worry and could manifest as a feeling of fear.

Instead of looking at the real problem, you make excuses. Or, just accept it as this is how I feel today. You wait for it to go away. Maybe it does, or you get focused on something else until the feeling switches.

Where Does the Fear Come From?

Our fear is a learned trait. Some people are full of fear and express it or deal with it through violence, bullying, or crime. Others become depressed, helpless, and live by fearful choices and indecision.

We all have our own way of dealing with fear because nobody really shows us how to handle situations that frighten us. If you're like most people, you've been taught that fear is a bad thing that you should avoid. When you feel afraid, you RUN! I think we've been running enough.

By focusing on weak spots, you empower your weaknesses instead of your strengths. Knowing how you confront your fear is the first step to getting through it. Do you procrastinate and put off tasks that you know should be done? If so, why do you put them off?

By breaking down your fear into steps or small stages, the power it has over you diminishes. What would you do if you had less fear? What if you could take your fear and turn it into a positive force that influences people and others to take action?

What would you do with your life today if you didn't have fear getting in the way?

We keep our fears alive by feeding into the fear-based mindset. Anxiety, worry, fearful thoughts, and paralysis all contribute to making you suffer. You can handle anything that comes your way. Believing that the fear is only temporary is a powerful tactic. And guess what?

It *is* only temporary.

As Buddha once said: *All things must pass.*

3

TEARING DOWN THE WALLS OF FEAR

"Fear is never a reason for quitting; it is only an excuse."

—Norman Vincent Peale, bestselling author of *The Power of Positive Thinking*

Facing your fears is hard work. There's a lot of uncovered emotional pain beneath the surface.

When you take apart the pieces of your life that are suffering from emotional turmoil, you will find that you've been surviving in the fear-based mindset. When you're in resistance mode, you're present in the fear-based mindset. When you free yourself to rise above your fears, you're making that shift into the power-centered mindset.

Here's a case example: A friend of mine (I'll call her Wendy) watched 3-4 hours of TV every night. She would watch anything that was on the tube. It didn't matter, as long as it took her mind off her problems, and the fear those problems created. She had a lot of credit card debt that she was unable to pay. Her fear identifier was her finances.

Wendy was never good at controlling her money because her father was a gambling junkie, and when she was a child, he had lost all the family money. Now Wendy was facing the same dilemma. She had creditors calling her and showing up at her home.

Every day, she would wake up with enough fear to kill an elephant and some mornings struggled to get out of bed. She just wanted to pull the covers over her face and black out the world. Wendy had other distractors as well, and one of them was online shopping, which only fueled her problems because she couldn't pay her current debts.

Resisting our fears doesn't make them go away. Avoiding our troubles just adds to stress and anxiety. This is why we need a logical flow to move from our fear-based center into a positive center that sets us free.

One of the biggest causes of stress is unresolved issues in our lives. This could be a massive bill that isn't paid or a difficult relationship we're not dealing with.

When we struggle to establish a solution for the situation causing stress (that also heightens our fears), we remain stuck in the fear-based side. Once this happens, attempts to find a way out are difficult because all our choices magnify the fear.

Trapped in the fear-based zone, all the doors we see lead to more fear. We need to find that one door that can give us the way out.

Our fears are derived from situations that appear beyond our control. Change is one of the things that most of us are afraid of in the beginning—until we actually do it.

Switching to a new career is going to be fearful—until we get accustomed to it. Leaving a relationship is fearful—until we actually do it. Fear of failure is frightening—until we've had some big failures that desensitize our fear.

Handling Resistance

We resist the circumstances that are emotionally painful. This can be anything from dealing with a situation at work, divorce, having financial trouble, and health problems.

When you try to find a solution and you're still thinking and acting within the boundaries of your fear-based zone, the solutions you come up with will fuel the problems.

For example, in Wendy's case above, instead of sitting down and discussing with the bank the best way to pay off her debt and create a payment plan for that (i.e., a power-based solution), she zones out and watches TV or keeps herself distracted through feeding into other activities with no connection to her problematic situation.

The payoff is that she can escape from reality; but the reality is that she can't escape from paying off her debts. The problem will continue to knock on her door until it's dealt with.

Resisting our fear is natural; it is actually the first stage of facing what scares us. The next step is how the situation is dealt with. It stems from a choice.

Will you bury your head in the sand and escape or take a (small) step toward dealing with it? One method will create greater stress down the road; the other will free you, and you'll develop better coping skills.

When it comes right down to it, all of us are afraid of change to some extent. For many, it's the fear of facing reality. We get immersed in our comfort zones; we build our little daily habits around this zone and get accustomed to the routine, the schedule, and our daily interactions with people.

Familiarity is a good feeling. It provides security and a safety net. The only thing that threatens our comfort zone is a new problem or circumstance that demands we change our routine—a sudden change that happens beyond our control.

When your fear-based center is introduced to a situation that it doesn't know how to handle, you're going to feel that tightening sensation in your chest. It's anxiety. You might experience helplessness or paralysis.

I had a friend who, when he was going through a traumatic time in his life, would experience paralysis of the mind so deeply that he couldn't walk. Literally, he would be laid up in bed for days.

Physically, there was nothing wrong with him, but his mind was struggling to deal with the situation that had been thrust on him. He was resisting heavily doing anything about it. When he overcame his fear-based mindset and switched from "fearful" to "fearless," an amazing transformation took place. He discovered that he could take action to get through his problem.

How did he overcome his fearful situation?

We talked about it and agreed that he couldn't just stay dormant. He was going to have to take an action, even the slightest movement, to get him moving forward. That first step might be a baby step but it's better than running the other way.

We broke down the steps he needed to take to get moving. You have to understand that this was someone who was mentally and emotionally paralyzed with the fear of "what's going to happen to me?" On an emotional level, he was convinced that whatever happened, he wasn't going to be able to deal with it.

In the end, he did what had to be done. The situation was taken care of, and after all the sleepless nights, and all the fear of not knowing what would happen, he survived. Most people associate their big situations with life-or-death scenarios.

Sometimes, we do have life-or-death situations, but most of them aren't.

When we're faced with a fearful situation, it's a natural course of action to resist what we fear. Just think of the last time you had something happen in your life that caused great fear. How did you react initially? Did you try to avoid the situation? Are you still avoiding it? Did you run? Procrastinate? Get drunk to forget about it?

Resistance is that wall of fright we have when we don't want to do something. Things are fine the way they are. Why disrupt it? We also resist because we may not know what to do. We ask, "How do I deal with this fear? I've never had this happen before. You're telling me to just 'do it,' but I really don't know where to begin."

I've dealt with many situations in my own life that required my courage to step up and take over. With every challenge that's new, you should remind yourself that this fear you have is not exclusive to just you. No doubt somebody has been through the same thing and they managed to make it out alive. You're not the only one who's afraid. It just looks that way.

Seven Reasons We Resist Fear

People handle their fear in many different ways. Most of us, whether subconsciously or not, will try to avoid fearful situations. This could be a new challenge where there's the possibility of failure, or it could be an uncomfortable situation we don't want to face. We might be procrastinating in taking action and do nothing indefinitely.

When we're afraid, there's a level of resistance that everyone has to break through. Our resistance to a situation depends on the level of fear we have in response to what scares us.

Here are seven reasons we resist facing our fears:

1. **We think our fear is exclusive.** Someone told me once that my problems were not new or original. Doesn't it feel most of the time like your fear is new and original? That somehow, you are the only one who has ever gone through this or is facing this situation?

   You might own your own fear, but the good news is that there's nothing you're facing that hasn't been handled before by someone else. This is good news because it means there's always a solution or case study you can find that will help you through anything.
2. **We think that the fear is bigger than we are.** This is the "I can't deal with this" phase. Believing that the fear is beyond our capacity to deal with, we become frustrated and look for ways to distract ourselves.

   As we'll see, distractions are convenient and keep the mind occupied. As soon as the distraction is finished, our minds return to the original problems. Only now, we feel guilty and more pressured to handle it!

   Fear is a constant emotion. It has no size or value. Two people could have the same situation and handle it completely differently. When we condition ourselves to handle these things, then we grow.
3. **We're afraid of the inevitable outcome.** I'll go into this in more detail later but fearing what might happen is a major obstacle. "What if I fail? What if it doesn't work out?" We run through every possible situation that leaves us filled with more self-doubt. Then, when a solution doesn't just appear, we're back to running and escaping from reality; this is our cycle when we're trapped in a fear-based mindset.

Every door we open offers another short-term solution.

To fix it, we have to stop getting "fixed". As soon as we buy into the path of least resistance, this pattern will continue to become our default habit throughout our lives.

The path of least resistance is the easy way out; it's where we can get enough distractions to keep us going forever. Full of mayhem and lacking any valuable solutions, the path of least resistance is tempting because of what it offers: an easy way to handle our fear. The path is easy because it provides a source of quick relief, but the long-term effects are more devastating.

4. **We deny that we're afraid.** How many times have we said, "I'm not afraid," but we really were? We rarely admit that something is scaring us.

   I hate tests. I'll have a certain level of fear when it comes to tests. Admitting I'm scared adds a level of confidence. I know I don't want to go through this. I'd rather be someplace else. So why am I doing this? Do I have to do this?

   In most cases, I could simply give up. That would be the easy thing to do. Walk away from the test. Leave the interview room before I'm called in. Giving up will assure my security and reduce the anxiety. But it won't get rid of the fear. It only strengthens it and molds it faster to my personality. My mind has now registered a new habit: I give up before facing the challenge.

   When we deny that we're afraid, we're boosting our level of fear. By admitting that we're afraid, we can say, "I don't like this, but I'll do it anyway. If I get through this, I'll be able to…" And then make a list of all the good stuff you have to look forward to when you take a stand.

5. **We take the wrong actions.** Another defense tactic we use to resist our fears is taking the wrong actions. This is similar to allowing distractions to happen, but instead of just doing whatever we feel like, we choose to take action, and then convince ourselves it's the right course of action—but it isn't.

   Instead of doing the work we should or could be doing, we opt to do something else instead. It's usually the easiest thing on our action list.

   Here's what you can do: write down the action that is causing you the most resistance right now.

   What would happen if you made this course of action your number one priority?

   Now, make it your priority and write out a list of three small actions you could take starting now. What's the first thing? Do it.

6. **We see the fear as something bigger than we are.** You can handle it. You just believe you can't. After you've handled it once, you'll be unstoppable.

   Here's the secret about all our nightmares—they're only as big as we decide they should be. How is it that some people can perform miracles in spite of their situation, and others can barely show up for a job interview?

   If you're reading this book, it's because you care about your well-being. I wrote this book because I care about your well-being, too.

   You can do this. There's nothing too big and no such thing as an immovable obstacle. You just need to figure out the right leverage to apply to move it. You'd be surprised that sometimes overcoming the biggest fears requires just a slight push.

7. **We think that the fear will just "go away" if we avoid it and do something else.** You can bury your fear, but it won't stay that way. Your life is meant to flourish and expand into something incredible. When you stop yourself from taking on new challenges, you put yourself in a vulnerable position. You're setting yourself up for a big fall the next time a big wave or challenge hits.

   Children who grew up in families that buried their problems and didn't discuss problem-solving solutions grow into adults who have a habit of running scared. They learn to deal with their emotional pain by creating elusive backdoors, engaging in compulsive lying, and forging addiction-based escape routes.

   We live in a world that's designed to keep us occupied 24/7. Some people fill their time with excessive TV watching. Others gamble or shop online. We get distracted as a way to cope with our pain. Because we struggle to deal with the painful emotions that facing fear brings, turning away from our fear is the best logical choice.

   When we turn off the lights in a room, the objects in that room are still there—even if we can't see them. For many of us, turning off our fear is like throwing a blanket over reality and saying, "I know you exist, but I don't want to see you."

   To move from your fear-based state of mind, you have to be willing to throw on the light switch and expose your fears to your consciousness. To repress what scares you is to open the door to a host of painful emotions: depression, worry, and agitation. If you live each day experiencing these emotions over and over again, you'll eventually make yourself sick.

Fear-Avoidance Tactics and Repression

Let's be honest for a moment. How often do people start each day by saying to themselves first thing in the morning, "Today, I'm going to tackle my fears and do the things I want, even if it's uncomfortable"?

If anything, we're conditioned to think and behave in just the opposite manner. We think, "Today, I'm going to play it safe, do my job, stay in my comfort zone, and hope that I'm not challenged too much."

Most people will do anything to avoid experiencing an uncomfortable situation. If only we knew that thinking, acting, and pushing against the "easy" way of doing things, we empower ourselves to a new level.

When you take the easy way, you take the long way. You might think you're getting away with something, but that's the illusion. Nothing could be further from the truth. Your freedom to create the life you want isn't going to be found by following all the safety rules. Only by going beyond them can you discover it. I'm not suggesting you take great risks that place you in danger, but I am suggesting this:

Ask yourself what it would take to live your life on your own terms free of fear. Imagine yourself taking on any obstacle and matching all resistance.

Why do most people fail? They give up when resistance gets in the way. The going gets tough and then we run.

Running from our fear is a conditioned response. We treat it as if there's something wrong with us.

So, how do people avoid facing fear?

We stay distracted.

Fear-avoidance gains a strong foothold in our lives. We

want to avoid being afraid, taking responsibility, and having to face our pain points. Confronting the things that scare us means putting our ego and confidence in the line of fire.

In today's busy society, being distracted has never been easier; we have digital media, television with more TV shows than we can watch in a lifetime and loads of food and snacks that fill us up without remorse.

For example, one of my distractors was Internet shopping. As an Amazon and eBay addict, I would spend hours just surfing the world's largest online stores. When I had anxiety, or there was something I'd rather avoid, I'd turn to the "easy" path of escape.

What distractors do you use? What triggers you to feed into this distractor?

Avoiding your fears is a natural path. There's nothing wrong with it if you want to stay hidden. When you give in to your distractions, it relaxes anxiety and makes you less fearful. But, only for the duration that you're doing something else

It takes your mind off the fear. It gets you into a zone where you don't have to think about anything else. This is your safety zone but it's not real. It's a temporary fix and nothing more. It exists only to provide relief in the now, but when you stop engaging in the activity, your anxiety and fear come back.

Most people will make themselves busy as a way of putting something off that they don't want to do. By being busy, you always have an excuse: "Oh, I was doing this, so I couldn't…"

Catching yourself in the act requires a level of awareness that must be developed. You can do this through three easy techniques.

Action Task

Make a conscious decision to be aware of the distractions you use to escape from emotional pain connected to your fears. Train your mind to identify your distraction patterns. Is it an addiction to a habit or a certain drug? Is it TV? We all have our methods of escape. Identify yours.

Resistance Test: The next time you're challenged with difficulty, take note of how you react. Do you try to find a solution? Are you excited to be challenged because it pushes you to grow?

We all have resistance to our fears. It's a natural reaction. Now, imagine taking that challenge and turning it into something real.

What's your favorite escape route?

Make a list of your escape routes you use to run. Identifying these is a powerful way to get motivated to doing something about it. Knowing your escape patterns brings out your conscious mind to block it. For years, I used video games to escape. I said it helped me to relax.

The truth is, it numbed my senses. Whenever something came up that I didn't want to deal with, I'd kill time with a game or TV. When I identified that, I threw out the games and turned off the TV. I would only watch something if I faced a challenge on that day and overcame it. Make yourself earn your reward. Earn it and you'll appreciate it a lot more.

Avoidance distraction keeps us stuck. Unlimited distractors surround us these days: TV, video games, or intoxicants that keep you from doing anything. If you're a procrastinator, you probably engage in these activities or you have your own outlet for distracting your mind. Identify what your avoidance tactics are and try to eliminate them or break the habit.

Resistance is natural. We fight against situations that frighten us. You can break your resistance by taking a small step—however minute—toward resolving the situation.

"Don't fear failure so much that you refuse to try new things. The saddest summary of a life contains three descriptions: could have, might have, and should have."

—Louis E. Boone

4

CHOOSING TO BE COURAGEOUS

"Your time is limited, so don't waste it living someone else's life. Don't be trapped by dogma—which is living with the results of other people's thinking. Don't let the noise of others' opinions drown out your own inner voice. And most important, have the courage to follow your heart and intuition."

—Steve Jobs

You could change your life in an instant if you made immediate choices toward worthwhile goals. Imagine where you'd be if you decided NOT to let fear get in your way of success. Where would you be if you decided that today, you were going to take your first step toward your dreams?

Now, what would it take for you to consider yourself to be a courageous person? We hear lots of stories of courageous people; those who climb the seven summits and risk their lives for others. We see courage in the movies and watch other people around us do the things we wish we could do.

This starts a comparison war with your fearful self. As you compare your lack of action and courage to people who are achieving far more than you ever have, your fear is given power to keep you stuck. You hear yourself saying excuses why you can't do things:

- I wasn't born that way.
- I'm not good enough.
- I've failed at most things I've tried.

I've spent most of my life delivering the same excuses to my subconscious mind. I always wanted to be more courageous because my fear always appeared more powerful than I was. When you believe in your fear over yourself, you give up the right to be courageous.

When I resisted or felt overwhelmed, it was never a time for courage. It was a time to run. It's a natural feeling. Animals flee when they're afraid. So do people. But we have control over our instincts. We have the power of choice and we can use that to our advantage.

By choosing to be a person of courage, you become a person of courage. You move out of fright mode. Your heart feels lighter. You take on the look of a determined person, and you shift your energy force.

Fear is a powerful emotion. You can use it to your advantage or let it run your life. You can sit in fear and let it drive you to feelings of self-doubt and low confidence, or you can accept it when it hits you and leverage it to do the thing that you're most afraid of doing. You can feel what your first instinct is and resist the temptation to do what it wants you to do.

Move yourself from a position of pain to a position of power. Listen to what your mind is telling you. Become aware of the voice that starts the dialogue without your permission.

You might think that you're not a courageous person, but let's look at that belief. You're sitting here right now, yes?

Chances are your life has had its share of difficulties. You've experienced suffering, emotional pain, loss, and grief in your life.

We're all trying to get through our lives and enjoy ourselves in the process. Life is meant to be fun… but for many, it isn't. If you are living a fearful lifestyle, it's hard for you to be brave or courageous. You want to hide and stay out of sight.

We're going to identify the actions you've taken in your life despite the fear and self-doubt. When I did this exercise, it occurred to me that I had been courageous most of my life. I just had the wrong idea of courage. I compared myself to real people who were successful, confident, and doing the things that I wanted to do. I looked at them as shakers and movers; I looked at myself as shaken and immobile.

My fear began with a thought. It was usually an image or idea that something bad was going to happen. By the time I got to work, the fear had expanded to a heightened sense of anxiety. I was told once that fear begins with future events that haven't happened yet or past events that are still unresolved.

It takes courage to live life. It takes more courage to face life's difficulties. It takes a certain level of confidence and courage to accept those difficulties as your own and overcome them.

Why Fear is Keeping You Stuck

I knew a woman once who was in a bad relationship. She had to get out of her marriage, but the thought of it put her into paralysis mode. She couldn't handle the idea of being on her own. She tried for years to adapt herself to the situation and even change herself to suit her husband's high demands. She was close to a breakdown and full of fear. She asked herself, "How will I survive? What if I can't make it on my own, and I have to crawl back to him? What if…?"

She was playing the "what if" game. All the roads were leading to fear and gloom.

There are two paths. The path to fearful living usually leads to one outcome: misery and more suffering. This generates more anxiety, stress, and paralysis. You feel trapped. But you're not trapped by the situation. You're trapped by your mind.

There's nothing in the external world that's keeping you stuck. It's an internal situation. Deal with it from there.

I sat down with this woman and asked her to write down all the steps she would have to take to leave her situation. She did, and there were about sixty items on the list. Then, I asked her to circle the action step that was the most challenging. She did. And next the action item that would be the easiest, that she could do right now. She identified the easiest thing on her list. Then she did it. It was as simple as making a phone call.

My friend continued to scroll through her list, tackling each action item until she got through half the items. By this time, she had serious momentum behind her. Her confidence level tripled she said. In just two weeks, she went from a paralysis condition to one of power just by working through her list, step by step.

If she had tried to do the most difficult thing first, she'd still be stuck. We need to start small to get some momentum going. Do what comes easy. You don't have to jump right in and take on everything at once. Within three months, this woman had her own apartment, she was working through the divorce proceedings, and, for the first time in her life, she was in control of her destiny.

How did she do this?

She identified what her fears were: the fear of being alone, abandoned, and not being able to make it on her own. All these fears were challenged. They appear real because she never questions them; when you strip it down and look at what scares you, the fear that masked your confidence shows itself. In many cases, your thoughts are fearful; they defeat your actions.

When you imagine yourself taking courage and facing the situation for the first time, resistance shows up in the beginning. You'll be tempted to wait for the right time or the perfect opportunity. But there's never a perfect moment. We wait for courage to show up, but it rarely does.

Courage and confidence are the result of working through the fear. When you decide to take total control of the situation and do something about it, you're activating your "courage" button. In other words, you're standing up and taking responsibility. By taking action despite the fear, you are taking the path towards true courage.

Now, how about you? Are you giving your fear permission to take over and run the show? How much of your fear is real? It might feel real to you, but nobody is projecting it onto you, are they? What thoughts are you having right now that are building the fear up? Do others perceive you as being fearful, or is it just you?

Taking Responsibility

I'll admit that I can be a hypocrite at times. As a father, I try to teach my children the importance of responsibility. I teach them to take care of their homework and chores before playing games or watching TV. When they do the difficult things first, they can enjoy their playtime more. I, on the other hand, have a powerful tendency to ignore my own fears and put off doing the stuff that could be done to reduce my own fear.

Instead of being courageous, there were many times I took to running and "leaving my mess behind" for someone else. This had caused more grief and suffering than I care to admit. It doesn't have to be this way. The reason I teach my children not to do this is so that they can hopefully suffer less as they get older.

Being courageous is about being responsible for the mess on your own side of the fence. Nobody else is going to take care of your problems, unless you pay them to do so.

The fear is yours if you want it.

People will project their fears onto you every day. You hear about it through the media and from your friends. How you choose to accept it is up to you. Will you reject fearful propositions or accept it as the truth? You have a choice in any given situation.

You can take responsibility for what happens in your life; or you can give it up and fall into the easy way of "avoiding" and "running" from your fears. This life is yours. You can choose to do what you want at any given moment. Once you know and accept this, it empowers you to act with courage.

Here are two strategies you can do to get more courage:

1. **Stop blaming others.** The quickest way to give away your power is to blame another person for something you had total control over. This is the quick and "easy" way to escape responsibility. Although it feels justified and right, pointing the finger diminishes your ability to handle life on life's terms. As the old saying goes, "When you point a finger at someone, there are three fingers pointing back at you."

I know people who never accept responsibility for their mistakes. They look to blame the first person they can find, and then seek to prove that it was really their fault while disowning any part of the problem.

These same people also live in constant fear. They are always on edge. They have limited comfort zones and panic if they step one inch outside of them.

You can avoid this if you step up and face your mistakes right away. Look for opportunity where you can help others to deal with their mistakes. Finger pointers think they win every time they get off the hook and everyone else takes the heat, but it is an illusion for them.

Be a model of honesty and, like I teach my children, if you did it that is okay. Just owning it makes you brave.

2. **Own your emotions.** When we're dealing with our fears, our emotions have a powerful role. It's a struggle to deal with our worry, stress, fearful thoughts, and anxiety. These are not fun to face up to. It isn't any wonder people would rather flee than fight.

   When we are paralyzed because we don't know what to do, the emotion can be overwhelming. The mind can actually begin shutting down.

   I handle this by walking through the process. Our emotions can be handled when we question their validity. If you're worried about something, and this is allowed to manifest into something bigger, it's because thoughts are permeating your mind and taking over. Doesn't it feel at times like you're under the power of an external force? When your thoughts produce anxiety, it seems like this is destined to be your life.

   The good news is that you're in absolute control of your

emotions at all times. It doesn't feel that way, but you are. This is very liberating. To know that I can choose my own thoughts means that I can eliminate worry at will. When I am having a bad day, and the world is a dark cloud, it's *my* dark cloud. I can own every feeling I have.

We're the creators of misery and happiness. Sadly, many people wait for someone else to make him or her happy, or to take away their miserable state. We can catch ourselves saying things like, "Well if only she would change, then I'd be happier."

Relying on other people to make you better is putting too much pressure on the other person. It's also unrealistic. Chances are that most people are thinking about their own happiness and are not always concerned about yours. You want to be more peaceful? You can produce the feelings and emotions to generate a peaceful state of mind.

You're not stuck in any relationship, job, or situation. It may seem that way, but you have a choice. The choice may not be an easy one, but if you choose to stay in a place that causes you suffering, then choosing to stand up to it will leverage your power. People are unhappy when they choose to *not* do something.

You want to live a different lifestyle because your present lifestyle isn't fulfilling? You can choose to live a different way. You have a choice in every situation that challenges you.

When you feel defeated, it's because you are not taking action. By choosing, we can overcome those feelings of helplessness and self-defeat.

5

PUSHING BACK AGAINST MEDIOCRITY

"People who are unable to motivate themselves must be content with mediocrity, no matter how impressive their other talents."

— Dale Carnegie, bestselling author of *How to Win Friends and Influence People*

We all live in our own comfort zones—safe havens that support our behaviors and habits. In these zones, we build walls of safety and convenience. This can lead to lethargy and poor habits that eventually defeat us. Rarely do we seek to change ourselves within these limitations. Instead, we've accepted our lives as they are. By accepting, you're willing to take anything that's given to you without question.

In the beginning of this book, I introduced two mindsets: the fear-based mindset, and the power-centric mindset. Mediocrity has its power in the fear-based center of our lives. It is one of the more powerful beliefs that we have about ourselves.

Mediocrity kills dreams and keeps people trapped. They try to drown out their pain with senseless activities, and a life of intoxicating numbness.

All of this, of course, is the basis for a fearful lifestyle. The subject of living in mediocrity goes beyond the scope of this book, but I have to bring it up to at least raise your awareness of its power and the illusion it represents.

Mediocrity isn't the life people desire; it's what they end up taking in exchange for a paycheck. Mediocrity is accepted by the masses because it's what everyone else is doing.

Henry David Thoreau, an American poet, once said: *"Most men lead lives of quiet desperation and go to the grave with the song still in them."*

We all desire to sing our song, live our dream, and rise above our own potential. Sadly, many people won't, but instead settle for less. Much less.

We believe that at our core existence, we're not worth enough to have or earn what we really desire. So we end up with less, much less. We take what we can get instead of going for what we desire. We end up trusting in our fears and developing weak habits that support a fear-based lifestyle.

In other words, inhibited by the fear of living, we live a mediocre lifestyle instead of the life we could have. This isn't living; it's surviving. People die every day without having ever played their music or sung their song.

When you believe in mediocrity, all the actions, thoughts, and behaviors you create are streamlined within this lifestyle. People live below their means not because they're incapable but because they have no faith or trust in themselves to live a great life.

When you streamline your actions and empower your fears to work with you, instead of holding you back, you'll become more confident and take intentional action consistently. We're born to explore and challenge the difficulties that life throws at us.

A life without obstacles is dull. What slows us down is when we act like those obstacles shouldn't be there, as though the universe were somehow conspiring against us to make life difficult.

The difficulty is not in the fear we have; it lies with our old conditioning and how to handle the fear. If we're not careful, we can buy into the lies that life should be easy, that we shouldn't struggle.

You might be stuck in the drudgery of a fatiguing job and think you can't leave. Or in a relationship that's smothering you, and you'd do anything to break free but, something's holding you back.

You want to take a stand, but instead, you find yourself groveling on the floor. You want a way out, and all you find is a room with locked doors and no way to leave. You want to be somebody, but "they" have convinced you that you're nobody, and this is where you belong.

Our fear-based self-reacts to sudden changes in habit or thinking. Mediocrity isn't a condition that we're born with; we grow into it from expectations placed by our environment. When we're treated as mediocre, we buy into the mediocre mindset.

We unconsciously decide that we're mediocre and begin to construct a life that proves it in every way. We model what we see and hear, and, if we try to be different, we'll get hammered back down.

Mediocre isn't what you are; it's a condition built on poor education. You're tricked into thinking you're not special, and you're taught this way of life by everyone around you who's caught up in the same system. It's nobody's fault; we can't blame our parents or teachers or mentors. They also have to deal with their own struggles of mediocrity.

A mentor of mine once summed it up perfectly. He called it "the science of mediocrity". In science, we rarely question the formulas (or what scientists call "laws"). For example, a proven formula is never wrong. It can never change its state, either.

When you think about your life's potential, can you honestly say that you have lived your life to the absolute best? Have you achieved your life dreams? Do you have that secret desire to do something wonderful with the rest of your time here, but you just can't get started? Do you listen to the voices of reason and believe everything they're telling you?

I've listened to these "chatterbox" villains most of my life and can honestly say that they're full of lies. These voices may be from the past or they come from your own personal demons. Whatever the source, you can adjust the content by taking over the messages they're sending. You will do what you believe in. You will act with authority on what you think and believe you're worth.

What we believe, we conceive.

Pay close attention to the language you are using when you communicate with your thoughts. Mediocre thinking is a habitual habit and reinforces our "average" way of life. When I say average I mean, acting and performing in a way that is below your potential because you are convinced that is what is expected of you.

I realized a long time ago I was feeding into my mediocre mindset with the thoughts and choice words I used to communicate with myself. When I started believing that I could do more, I did more. I got excited about what I could accomplish. I slept less because when you're fired up about your goals, you don't need as much sleep.

When you make the conscious decision to push out of your bubble, you trigger an emotional response that some people call "motivation". You start the snowball effect of going faster and doing more with each attempt. Before you know it, you're doing things that you once just dreamt of.

Mediocre conditioning begins early in life, usually in childhood when you learn to fear things for the first time. You hear people tell you to "be careful" or "don't do that, you'll get burned."

A life of mediocrity isn't something you're born into; it takes years of heeding the messages from everyone else. You form your limitations, create and establish the things that you're afraid of, and establish your level of success based on the environment you're raised in.

According to the definition of mediocrity by Merriam-Webster, mediocrity is:

> *"The quality of something that is not very good: the quality or state of being mediocre. A person who does not have the special ability to do something well."*

In a nutshell, someone who's not special, talented, has no real ability, and is low in quality.

Would you define yourself this way? If you answered yes, that's good. It's your first step to changing it.

If we judge our success by the talented musicians, artists, movie stars, rock icons, politicians, and people of general importance, mediocrity would define about 97% of the world's population. If that were true, what does that say about us? Are we a mediocre species by nature?

We're raised by mediocrity to believe that if we don't express any magical talent, we have nothing to really offer, and if we're not part of the royal family, our life is destined to be poor and boring. It's a system of beliefs impressed upon us further by an educational system that prepares people for jobs they end up not wanting anyway.

Mediocrity has its power in your deepest thoughts and beliefs; over the years, this conditions your habits to respond and adapt to mediocre ways. Your actions become a reflection of how you feel about yourself. Your level of happiness, satisfaction, and success in both personal and professional life is driven by your beliefs in who, what, and why you are.

Have you ever asked yourself why you do something that you really don't want to do? You find yourself stuck in situations and wonder how you got there. If you can trace back your patterns, you may see that you were following a system that has its beliefs established in your mind from many years back.

Now, how would you feel if you were to:

- Apply for a job you've always considered to be out of your league?
- Asked for something that you'd normally never ask for because you thought, *I'm just not worth it*?
- Eat at an expensive restaurant for the first time and not be afraid to have others wonder what you're doing there?
- Make a down payment on the dream house you've always desired?
- Live your life as a traveling entrepreneur?
- Say NO the next time you're told to do something you don't believe in doing?
- Decide that, five years from now, you're going to make a seven-figure income?

Mediocrity is a form of fear, and it's the most difficult form to assess because nobody else can decide for you if you're trapped in a mediocre lifestyle. Only you can do that. Only you can awaken your inner "dragon" to take charge, go out there, and make a bigger difference.

Your mediocrity mindset is the breeding ground for maintaining a level of consistent fear that keeps you where you are. When you stand against those beliefs and really question the why, you're taking a massive step. You're going to feel uncomfortable at first, almost "naughty," as if you might get caught acting up. That's just your fear-based center feeling the push.

When you become "aware" of the stuff trapping you, you'll feel a set of reactions take place. This is good. You want to make a conscious effort to move into your power-based center where you have a greater range of control.

One night, I made a list of all the ways I could continue to challenge the science of mediocrity.

Here's the list I made:

- Set a goal that is bigger than anything you've ever dreamed possible… and then, set out to accomplish it.
- Master something that nobody else is doing.
- Become a nonbeliever in past failures.
- Don't settle for what's left over—in fact, don't settle at all!
- Have a different plan than everyone else.
- Embrace your fear of failure and fail as many times as you can.
- Question your beliefs and really go deep to see if they're telling the truth about who you really are.
- Don't play it safe just because it makes others feel more comfortable.

- Push yourself a little further each day. Keep going forward.
- Continue to learn and educate yourself.

I want you to add to this list. Get started today on dismantling the illusion that you're just an average person with little to offer. I'm not suggesting you have low esteem, but all of us are somehow trapped into thinking we're less.

Mediocrity has its limits. The imagination does not. Challenge your limitations because you own them. You control them. You're not mediocre, but your actions today will speak for themselves.

Push back against any mediocre thoughts that keep you below what you know you're capable of. Don't settle for less, but push ahead for more.

6

GATHERING YOUR TRIBE OF FEARLESS WARRIORS

"You are the average of the five people you spend the most time with."

— Jim Rohn

One of the elements of growing into deeper awareness of your fears is that you begin to recognize the fear in everyone else, too. You can spot all the subtleties and diversion tactics that people employ to escape from their emotional pain.

This is frightening at first, and you'll want to revert back to being "blind." I encourage you to stay aware and watch the world around you. You're not only managing your own fear but, you expend a great deal of energy either absorbing the fear of other people or, in your own fearful moments, put it back onto others.

The World of Fearful People

Most people are living through their fear, and they don't even know it. They're stuck in mediocre positions in their jobs, and when they're done for the day, they go home to watch TV or kill time. When they communicate, their words are full of fear and self-doubt. They'll only take actions that are guaranteed to have viable outcomes. They have given up on their dreams because the reality they're now living in has defined who they are and what they're capable of.

We all know these people. They're our friends, family, and coworkers. As much as we love them and want to help them, self-discovery and the path to freedom is for the individual to discover for himself or herself.

When you decide to change the course of your life, one of the first things you'll notice is that not everybody is equipped to deal with your new changes. They're going to resist you and anything you're trying to do. Not because they don't like you but because it's a threat to their security.

If you try to talk about a new skill you learned or something outside the usual chitchat of the life you're escaping from, they'll change the subject and talk about things you used to be into. But you've moved on. You're no longer interested.

This is why you might need a new tribe of friends. I'm not saying you have to abandon your old friends. They'll always be there, but not the way that you want them to be.

When you make higher-level choices that break away from the old patterns and ways of doing things, something is getting left behind. In most cases, it's a job you've outgrown or a relationship that's holding you back.

Our fear can keep us in these situations indefinitely if we don't break clean. When I was in my early 20s, I was in a relationship with a girl who was holding me back. She wanted to settle down and get serious. I wanted to explore the bigger possibilities of life and see what was out there.

My desire and drive made the decision, but it took almost two years before I could walk away completely. I was used to the comfort of the relationship, and my fear of being alone was keeping me in a situation that I was growing to resent.

When I pushed past all that and decided to throw away the comfort of staying in a relationship that was keeping me stuck, I moved on. I went and did all the things that I dreamed about.

Preparing for Resistance

Be aware of your friends who are fearful people. They worry about their future and they're sticking to their fears without taking risks. When you have a great idea and you need to tell them about it, there's that cautionary voice of "You don't know what you're getting into" or "I've heard bad things about that system."

You see, many people are operating without awareness from their fear-based center. They're still stuck in the old system. They believe in limitations and are wary of risks or going too far. They're your family, friends, and people at work. You might love them and want to help them too, but when you decide that you're changing the way things have always been, expect resistance.

The question you need to ask yourself is, how much time am I spending with them? The people you associate with every day become a part of your life, and they define you in many ways. Make sure they're the right people.

Like attracts like, so if you're sitting down and having complaint sessions with your buddies, this is what you can expect more of in the future: complaints, whining, and conversations that generate more fearful ideas. Nothing is solved, and the only thing shared is an hour of negative speeches.

When you're past the fear-based mindset, you can rise above this action. When you do, people will ask you, "What's your problem? I thought you liked hanging out with us." Or, the classic return: "Oh, you're too good for us now. Is that it?"

Be prepared for resistance from others. You may have to distance yourself from the usual crowd. This isn't to say you need to dump all your friends and people who don't "get" the new you, but when you make that conscious decision to no longer accept a certain norm, you're rocking the boat and people will get wet.

Your tribe of heroes is the people in direct line with your actions, goals, and ambitions. If you're a writer like I am, you're surrounded by a positive group of supportive people who you can bounce ideas off of and share your thoughts. They're a part of your tribe.

Many of our fears are not really created by us as much as the messages we get from others. One person's low confidence and self-doubt can rub off on another. The negative weak words and actions of other people create a deeper exposure to fear. It becomes a group collective.

If you hang out with fearful people, you learn to fear the world. You'll hold onto this fear and carry it with you well into your old age if you don't change it. "Birds of a feather flock together" and this is the truth.

People with positive energy and aspiring goals are most likely not going to hang around with those who are wasting time on worthless tasks. Negative people will invariable seek out like-minded people.

Finding Your Niche Support

Your tribe of fearless warriors are the people who are there for you when you need them. They're the ones who push you to rise to your greatest potential. They'll be there when you're ready to make that BIG leap to the next level. They know what you can do, and they want you to succeed more than anything.

They won't hold you back because to do so would deny who you are. We all want that "dream team" of people who could be there to support us in times of difficulty; the men and women who've been there and are not afraid to go through it again with someone struggling.

Remember this: Your success is a mirror of the five people you spend the most time with. So, who are they? Do they inspire you and lift you up? If not, what's your relationship to them? A good friend of mine, who had been married for 20 years, left his wife after realizing that she couldn't and wouldn't support his dream to have his own business.

He tried to make a go of it in the marriage, but she was interested in just his day job that would bring home a paycheck. A personal business would cost money to set up, things would be tight for a while, and she wouldn't have the luxury of living with a steady wage earner and expecting a weekly paycheck. He had two choices: stick with the day job he hated or divorce.

He took a chance, pursued his dream, and never looked back, and he's now running his own business and doing what he always wanted to do. His wife found someone else to marry who had a steady job to support her lifestyle and he's now running his own business and doing what he always wanted to do.

You need to seriously reflect upon and observe the people you spend your time with. Outside of family, who are your friends and acquaintances? Are they just passersby or do you have real relationships with fearful friends? If so, what can you do? Remember, you can only change yourself in any given situation.

I've been in many situations where I tried to change something about myself, but every time I would get together with the people who saw risk-taking and change as some kind of threat to their survival, I would end up doubting my purpose in life. I would be dragged back into another conversation about how hard life is and listen to all the reasons (i.e., excuses) why life's so hard. It was like resetting my success meter back to zero every time I put myself in that situation.

Be observant of the people who are trying to hold you back. It seems like they're engaging in some sort of sabotage. They may ask you, "Why are you doing this?" or "What's gotten into you?" We have to realize people are still struggling with their own demons and personal trials.

If they aren't ready, the best thing you can do is leave the door open for them. Maybe someday, they'll join you. But when you stand up for yourself and know that nothing can hold you back, the choice is imminent.

Like my friend who left his marriage, if he had stayed, he would have taken the easy path in the short run. In the long run, he would have realized one day that he had passed up his opportunity for success. When he took a chance and joined up with some business partners who became part of his tribe, it changed his entire social circle.

You have to know whom to cut loose; you need to decide who's going to join your fearless warrior campaign. You need to know and trust the personal traits your tribe of people has so that when you find them, you'll know right away.

That's the great thing about today's technology: We can expand our relationship universe without leaving home. Your tribe of warriors is out there, and you can find them if you try. I've gathered my warrior tribe over the past two years, and it has changed everything.

Dealing with Change in Relationships

When you start to move away from your fear-based mindset, you'll also be leaving behind the people who are still stuck there.

Picture this: there are two doors in front of you in a long hallway. Behind door #1 is your freedom and your new tribe of supporters and people who love what you're doing with your life. They want you to take that big leap and break free.

Behind door #2 is the old way of thinking and doing and being. The power behind that door is what's keeping you stuck. But you still have some friends there, and they're holding on tightly, begging you not to go.

You do have to make a choice. You can't have everything. For years, I was reaching for one door but being held back by the other. You're either going to stay in your fearful state (e.g., scarcity, limitations, negativity) or move into the power-based center (e.g., abundance, opportunity, positive influence).

This doesn't mean that you have to "get rid of" the people who have walked with you on the journey up to now. The best we can do is leave that other door open for them. It's an invitation. When they're ready, they can walk through it.

Remember, shifting out of your fear zone is going to rock the boat. You'll feel empowered to make tough love choices some people will resist. Your old tribe doesn't want you to change, not because they don't care about you but because they're afraid of being left behind. The door is always open if they want to walk through.

You'll find this level of resistance in most of your everyday interactions: with friends; with family; and at work. You'll be tempted to be pulled back into the fear zone because that has been your comfort zone for many years. If this happens, it's okay. Once you break away from your fear-based mindset, it will be easier to continue moving further away from it.

This is especially true in relationships (e.g., marriages, romantic relationships) when one person discovers something new, and the other partner is threatened by this new voyage of discovery. One person is on a growth path, and the other isn't ready to walk that road yet. When this happens, you must either persevere and grow together or break up.

Your Greatest Warrior in the Tribe

Try to find a mentor or accountability partner whom you can lean on for support. A mentor can be there to guide you through rough times when you're struggling. It's someone higher up the development chain who can provide answers, make suggestions, or, sometimes, just tell you how it is.

Modeling a mentor is a powerful way to leap forward. This person would be a leader, personal development coach, or a community leader.

When you're stuck in a fear-based mindset, you can break free by modeling the behaviors and attitudes of successful, positive people. If you want to act and be a certain way, find the people, leaders, and coaches who are acting and being in a manner you strive for.

Accountability partners are powerful too. These are the

people you can interact with in social network groups or someone in your community. It could be a co-worker or a friend. You might be taking a course together and need to pair up to hold each other responsible for making goals and completing tasks.

I make weekly calls to my accountability partners. After the calls, I feel confident and filled with positive energy. Any fears or worries we have about something can be discussed in a conversation.

Your accountability partner is generally someone who is in the same boat as you and striving to achieve similar goals. Most people who are adamant about accomplishing goals and making serious changes in their lives are hooked up with an accountability partner, a mentor, or both.

Search for an accountability partner and hold weekly calls, or a meet-up someplace. Discuss where you are with things, and the steps needed to help each other out.

Build your tribe of heroes by connecting with people who are positive and have a high level of influence in your life. Be aware of how these changes are affecting others around you and adapt accordingly. You can tell them what you're doing, and, if they're interested, they may join you. If not, the door is always open when they're ready.

"Worrying about scarcity is our culture's version of post-traumatic stress. It happens when we've been through too much, and rather than coming together to heal (which requires vulnerability) we're angry and scared and at each other's throats."

—Brene Brown,
bestselling author of
Daring Greatly

7

ADOPTING A "NOTHING TO LOSE" MINDSET

"Never let people who choose the path of least resistance steer you away from your chosen path of most resistance."

—David Goggins,
bestselling author of *Can't Hurt Me*

I was once a very indecisive person. Before making any decisions, I would weigh all the risks. I would balance the risk with the reward, and I would also consider the losses if my choices went bad.

I would always weigh the outcome heavily. But, what would stop me from taking a specific action that could change my life for the better was the fear of loss. If I failed and made the wrong choice, I'd lose something very precious to me.

The fear of loss is the all-consuming excuse we employ that keeps us stuck in doing the same things and not trying anything new.

It always comes back to this disempowering question: *what if I fail?*

Yes, you might. You probably will fall down a few times. Someday soon, you're going to die as well. When we're on our deathbeds, will we still be asking that same question of all the things we never tried: "What if I fail?"

By not choosing, you're choosing by default to stay where you are. By delaying a decision that will have an outcome, you're putting your life on hold...indefinitely. You can only create change or get unstuck if you take action.

Are you waiting for someone else to decide? They will, but it will rarely be in your favor. If you fail to decide, someone else will always be willing to choose for you...and you lose your personal power. Your own hand disempowers you.

It's fear of the outcome that stops us from acting on a decision. We fear losing something, but ironically, in many cases we fear losing the things we don't even have.

For example: My friend hated his job, but he was afraid of going on a job interview with another company. When I asked why, he said, "What if they reject me, or they tell me that my skills aren't enough for the position? What if I take the job, it doesn't work out, and then I have to quit? I'll have no job opportunities to fall back on. What if they stick me in the HR department and...?"

My friend was stuck in the "what if" game that trips everyone up when it comes to making decisions. When we are focused on the possible negative outcomes that are inevitably a risk, we worry about what will happen. What if it doesn't work out? What if they don't like me? What if I lose money? What if I have to start over again?

There's no such thing as a perfect decision. If you wait until the timing is right, the moment is perfect, or all the stars are in perfect alignment, you'll wait forever.

Then, somebody else will make the decision you didn't. They'll gain what you walked away from.

But the point isn't that you win or lose by deciding. You won't empower your fear if you ONLY get a good and positive outcome. You empower yourself by taking action *in* the decision. Making the decision *is* the victory.

This is true, not only if it works out but, taking action toward something and knowing that you'll probably fail at it *is* winning. Not just doing it and expecting to win but doing it and accepting what happens. That's the start of courage. This simple truth is where the power is. The outcome is irrelevant.

Forget about the rest.

Make a choice and you can let go of the rest. You can't predict the outcome of future decisions regardless of how logical or perfect they may seem. I've made choices that, at the time, seemed like golden eggs, and I couldn't lose, but I did. I've lost thousands of dollars on a financial choice that I was convinced would be a winner.

Would I have made the same decision if I had suspected there would be a chance of losing my money? Probably not, but without a commitment to anything, you can't get anything done. You need to commit to the course and stay on track. Not all of it is going to end up being good, but if you hold back and do nothing, you'll never know how far you could have gone.

You will succeed the moment you make your decision. Forget about the outcome. Focus on the moment, and the energy of your intentional choices.

It's like this: there will always be fear when it comes to making a choice, and the bigger the decision the larger the fear is looming over you.

Disempowering Choices

I want you to think about these three questions:

1. What would you do, starting today, if you had no fear about making decisions, taking action, or future outcomes?
2. What would you do if you absolutely knew that there was no way you could fail?
3. What would you do if you had total confidence in your ability and skills, and no fear?

It's not easy to think about. That's because most of the time, we're subconsciously thinking, analyzing, and balancing the good with the bad. We weigh the fear of taking action with the "What if" scarcity way of thinking.

Here's an example. Instead of imagining what could be (i.e., what you could gain) our minds are wired to fear the outcome of losing. What do I have to lose? And worse yet, Can I afford to lose this?

We're defeated by our own fear the moment we try to move against the resistance. It becomes like a maddening circus…in our minds! You want to do this, but what if…

- What if I lose money?
- What if the new situation is worse than the one that I'm in now?
- What if I'm still unhappy?

The result is you either fail to decide, or you make a half-hearted decision. You leave the door open in case it goes south, and you need an escape plan.

Instead of committing to your course of action and going

for it, you negotiate with your fear. You have one eye on your goal, but the other is watching out for danger, and if something goes wrong, you flee.

The first step is to recognize that you're wired to fear everything. We are taught from a young age that the world is a scary place. It's in the news every day. It exists inside and outside our homes. Fear rules and we're the servants.

If we fail to recognize that we are buying into the lies fear brings then our lives become ruled by circumstances. We become programmed into thinking and trusting in a system that keeps us trapped.

You are the master of your life. Fear is not your master but a servant to your higher choices. By adopting a "Nothing to Lose" mindset, you can program your mind for a new course of action.

You'll be met with strong resistance from your fear-based mind. It doesn't like new concepts. It prefers a safety net of rules, regulations, and strict adherence to emotional control. You can turn that around in your own mind.

Now:

- Make as many decisions as you can. Let go of the outcome.
- Nothing changes in life unless you make hardline choices and decisions.
- Let go of the idea that you are going to either win or lose. Deciding is assuming responsibility and taking charge of your life.

For every 9 out of 10 decisions, you might fail—but what about that one decision that really counts?

8

LEARNING TO FAIL BEFORE YOU SUCCEED

"Try a thing you haven't done three times. Once, to get over the fear of doing it. Twice, to learn how to do it. And a third time, to figure out whether you like it or not."

—Virgil Thomson

F. That was on the majority of my tests from math class in high school. Written in big red ink.

F as in Failed.

Worse yet—the other kids were shown my failure because our teacher, who wanted to set an example of what happened when you didn't study (and I'll admit that I didn't study much). She would post the failed tests at the back of the room for one week.

The smart kids would snicker, and the ones who barely passed were thankful they had been spared the humiliation. I wasn't one of the smart kids; I was mediocre, and I hated it.

I didn't like school very much. It wasn't the work or the environment; it was the expectations. I struggled from a young age to do well, and I never could. Eventually, I came to accept my own mediocrity and that I just wasn't smart. When you believe in your limitations, they set the standard for your success or failure throughout your entire life, unless you correct your internal compass.

When you fail at most things, you develop the attitude that failure is inevitable. By accepting and expecting to do poorly, you will do poorly. Your attitude is conditioned to see a failure as something you should be punished for.

This is how many things in society are arranged. You get praised for succeeding and are promoted or given more money; if you fail, you get demoted and something is taken away. It's the game of plus and minuses.

I got used to seeing my test paper on the back wall of that classroom. In the beginning, it bothered me; I had that feeling of shame that I wished would go away. I hated walking into class and knowing that my paper was the only one on the back wall. It didn't inspire us to improve. It conditioned us to avoid failure.

"You see what happens if you don't succeed? We scare you into doing well." But the experiment backfired. I eventually didn't care. In fact, I would fail on purpose just to show my teachers I didn't give a shit. My defiance was my victory.

I never learned the lessons about failing. Most of us students were taught to avoid doing poorly. You fail and you get an F. You do well and you get a treat. It was cut and dry.

Over the years, we've learned that failing isn't good. If you fail, you're letting down the team. You won't make it. The only way to get ahead in life is to have that winning edge, that unbeatable strategy.

By fearing failure, we grow reclusive. We avoid risks. We take the easy way and the path of least resistance. We become accustomed to the mediocrity of living beneath our true potential because success is reserved for those who can perform well.

If you failed miserably in your life and were ridiculed for your efforts, you may have developed resentment toward success. This happens when you're taught that failure is not tolerated. Instead of learning to fail so that you can build on success over time, the message you receive is that you must hit the mark every time. You must be perfect in what you do, or don't do it at all.

When I was a kid, I wanted to play the piano. I was told I had no musical ability. So, I never played. I believed in the opinion of one man, and, to this day, I always had the desire to play. In fact, when I look at a piano, I still feel that draw to sit down and play it—even though I can't read music. Don't let others dictate what you're capable of.

Don't let the fear of others stop you from doing what you love. It's okay to fail. It's the only way to learn. By not doing it right, you end up doing it really well. Failing is your greatest teacher. By learning to fail, you can make improvements to your approach and strategy.

Learning to Fail In 4 Steps

1. Failure is a perspective. There's an expression for when you fail at something: "Two steps forward; three steps back." A good mentor taught me that failing is never taking a step back. When you learn how *not* to do something, it's equally as important as doing it right the first time.

But what's even better is, the people who will come after you and attempt the same thing can avoid making the mistake if they follow your model. A pioneer who takes that first leap is never seen as a failure but an innovator.

Was **Steve Jobs** a failure? He quit college. Apple fired him after Jobs mistakenly (by his own admission) hired John Sculley. He launched numerous product failures such as Macintosh TV and The Apple Lisa that cost the company millions. Steve Jobs passed away in 2011 and Apple is now worth over 710 billion. Not bad for a garage startup.

Author **J. K. Rowling** failed for years as an author. She was rejected twelve times by traditional publishers and told not to quit her day job. She kept going. The Harry Potter series has sold close to half a billion copies worldwide. J. K. Rowling also quit her day job.

Walt Disney was fired from his job at Kansas City Star and told he lacked imagination. He then created such animation masterpieces as Snow White and Peter Pan. The Walt Disney Company is now ranked #11 for the world's most valuable brands.

Colonel Sanders was fired and rejected from dozens of places before his chicken recipe was sold. There are now 18,875 KFCs around the world. To this day, the recipe is still unknown.

Thomas Edison failed thousands of times. He went on to develop over 1,000 patents in his lifetime—including the lightbulb.

L. Frank Baum's *The Wonderful Wizard of Oz* was rejected so many times by publishers that he had a thick binder of rejection letters that he titled *A Record of Failure. The Wonderful Wizard of Oz* has been translated into over 50 languages, and tens of millions of copies have been published in dozens of countries. The movie was just as popular as the book. It's been estimated that over one billion people have seen *The Wizard of Oz,* more than any other movie.

Failure is everywhere. You might be thinking, "Oh, but those people were different. They had talent and motivation. They had great ideas. I don't have any of that."

Talent is really a lot of hard work and making mistakes until you get it right. Forget about the "prodigy" symptoms. It rarely exists. The successful people you see and hear about every day learned to suck it up and keep going. They learned to fail no matter what the naysayers threw at them. You can do the same.

If you give up because someone said you don't have what it takes, you're giving your power over to that person. You're selling yourself short. Do this once and you'll always do it.

Learning to fail is about accepting the truth. I have to fail first to get to where I want to be. You need to fall down before you win the race.

2. You're learning to disempower perfection. Perfectionistic thinking is a mindset that states, "I'm okay, as long as I get this right... the first time." The fault is that *nobody* gets it right the first time. Perfection has its power in the fear-based mindset. Perfection keeps more people stuck than any other form of resistance.

But who's perfect? I know a lot of people who *think* they are. I have struggled with perfectionism for most of my life, born out of the belief that failure is bad, we should avoid it, and we need to be perfect in everything we do.

When you're operating from a perfectionistic mindset, you're going to have a lot of fear crop up when things go wrong.

And things will go wrong. Mistakes will be made. People will get hurt or angry. They might even criticize you for screwing up. Perfectionism is a tool that fearful people use to measure the value of everything around them. If it's perfect, it has value; if it isn't, it's useless.

People who are raised in a critical environment develop perfectionistic attitudes. They become paralyzed by it.

The fear of trying new things is so overpowering that they do nothing. It's the biggest flaw and a lie. You might think that you have to be perfect but rarely does anyone else have as high expectations as you hold for yourself. If they do, it's their problem and not yours.

You can disempower your perfectionistic ways by putting stronger emphasis/focus into achieving simple steps. If you're writing a book and you fear your writing isn't perfect with perfect prose and grammar, write a sentence and let it sit for a while. Then do it again and again. Break down the action into the smallest task possible.

You get into perfection mode when the task or ideal is looked at from a microscopic view. You think about all the finer details involved in getting something accomplished. This is when you procrastinate for fear of starting something. Just take the simplest task you can and focus on it. It won't be perfect, and nobody's around to criticize you for it.

The more you start to do; the easier things will flow. You'll reduce your fear by doing it—even if it's a simple task. You can create a list of tasks focused on a goal that you've always wanted to achieve and take action toward something you feel driven to accomplish.

Decide to focus on one thing each day that will move you closer to your goal. Every little step counts. My definition of "making progress" is handling the stuff that matters most in small chunks. Not trying to do it all at once but making baby-step achievements every day.

This is the perfect opportunity to become aware of that "nasty voice" that's telling you "You're no good. You never have been. What are you doing?" It's the voice of the past and it's full of fearful words and bad influence. It operates on silent mode most days and you don't even recognize it's there. Be conscious of its undertone. It's full of lies.

3. You learn from what doesn't work. Nobody does it right the first time. That's what learning's all about. It's our expectation to get it right the first time that holds us back from succeeding every time. If you expect perfection, you'll end up thinking about doing it, but you won't actually attempt anything.

Your mind will create the illusion that as long as you don't try it, you can't fail at it. If you follow this philosophy, you can't learn from what doesn't work. You can empower your fear of failure by learning from what the failure is teaching you.

When I started writing books, I sucked at writing. My prose and grammar were all over the place, and the sentences were clunky and full of clichés. My writing still isn't perfect, but it's better than it was. Over the years, I've learned to adopt a certain writing style, but this only came with practice. You may not be a writer, but you might play sports or music, or you may be trying to launch an online business.

Trust me: you'll make a lot of errors. The only people who don't are those who are sitting in a comfort zone, too afraid to try. But they'll criticize those who foul up. For years, I was afraid of publishing anything because of criticism. But now, I can accept it as part of the course.

Learn from what works. Learn even more from what doesn't. Adjust your strategy and try a new one. Keep adjusting. Keep trying. Keep pushing through.

4. You build up a resistance to making mistakes. You can learn to fail by doing it. People who give up after the first few bumps are conditioning themselves to give up when it gets tough. To succeed at anything, be prepared to not succeed.

Remember that there's no such thing as "two steps forward three steps back" when a failure is another step toward success. You can desensitize yourself to making mistakes. In school, I numbed myself to failing so much that I no longer cared. Then I started to do better. But I had to accept failing first. I had to get used to it. Then I decided to make a difference.

You will succeed at whatever it is you desire if you stick with it and move. Be like a boxer in the ring; don't just stand there and wait to get hit. Roll with the punches. You might get knocked down, but you only lose if you stay down.

Look at failure as a necessary part of your journey to success. When a ship sets sail, it's constantly adjusting its course. It has to or else it'll end up on the rocks. Our failures and mistakes are all those little adjustments we have to make along the way.

There's nothing to fear when you look at failure as a necessary element for personal empowerment. If you're not afraid each day, then you're probably not doing enough to scare yourself.

Failure is an attitude. When you fail, it doesn't mean you're falling back. You might stumble, but you're always moving forward as long as you're doing something.

Failure is an opinion and not a concrete fact. Steve Jobs failed many times. So, did thousands of other "failures" that changed things and made their dreams come true.

Disempower your perfection by focusing on small tasks that matter. Stay in the present moment. Turn off "brain notifications" that say you have to be perfect at this.

Failing is part of the process and a necessary one. Learn to fail and do it as often as you can.

Don't let failure be your excuse to give up.

9

SAYING NO TO SELF-DOUBT

"There's always that moment of doubt before you take courage, before you jump off the edge into the unknown."

— Anonymous

Self-doubt is a term that describes a lack of trust in oneself. The truth is, many people doubt themselves when they must take intentional action and move against the obstacles that are holding them back. Their self-doubt isn't the barrier people think it is; it's a necessary step that they must work through before they achieve success.

You don't have to wait for confidence to show up before you do something that scares you. You don't need courage before you act; you gain confidence after you overcome your moments of doubt. Confidence is like motivation; if we wait for/depend on its arrival, we could spend a lifetime waiting.

The confidence comes when you act; if the first step is self-doubt in any situation, the next step builds your confidence. You feel better about what you can really do when you do what needs to be done first.

If you have doubt when you're facing a new challenge, that's good. It's a sign that you're stepping out of your comfort zone.

You're worried that you could fail. You risk losing something, and by challenging that doubt, you push it out of the way. Believing in your doubts and giving up empowers your sense of failure; you leverage your power when you move against it.

Self-doubt is always temporary. As soon as you get out there and do it, it's diminished. It might show up again the next day, but that's because you're pushing the envelope again, going further, breaking out of the fear-based zone. Think about anything you tried the first time and you'll remember that you were loaded with self-doubt.

- Can I do this?
- Should I do this?
- What if I don't do this?
- What if I fail my first time?

The loop comes back to the fear of failing. It's the old antagonist of every success story. The fear of failure is a lack of faith in yourself to succeed. If you buy into its power, you'll always have it.

People who are afraid to leap fear the unknown. You'll hear the voices of people warning you against it: They may say, "You'd better not jump. Nobody has ever made it this far." No—some did, and they're the better for it.

They may say, "That's risky. I know so many people who have died trying." Yes—and I know many who died without trying but wished on their deathbed that they had tried.

They may say, "You don't know what's out there." That's true. But if I just sit here in the same place, doing what I've always done, I'll *never* know what's out there.

You never know what's out there until you go looking for it.

When I finished college 20 years ago, I made a daring

choice. The economy at the time was depressed, and there weren't many jobs in my field. A friend of mine who lived out west in Vancouver suggested I move there because the place was booming, and everyone had work.

Now, I come from a small town, and I'll be honest; I had never traveled or moved very far from home. In fact, I was pretty set on staying where I was. I had a girlfriend, and we were madly in love. I was going to marry her, live in a small house, and have kids and a couple of dogs.

I spent most of my days drinking in the local pub and enjoying the life. I didn't have a lot of ambition other than getting a job and staying in my hometown.

But my friend's offer was on my mind. Then, he sent me pics of the city. My initial fear of leaving home turned into a deep interest.

This changed into a powerful drive to do something more with my life than just sit around, watching life pass me by. The more I thought about it, the more excited I started to feel, but there were lots of voices in my head at play. They sounded like this:

- "What if you get out there and you hate it? You'll have to come home a failure."
- "What about your girlfriend, and the house and two dogs you talked about?"

The voices wanted me to stay. They wanted the easy life. They wanted to believe the fear. But I knew that wasn't an option.

I told my parents about my idea. They knew I wanted to do more with my life. I knew that too. There was a force inside me that wouldn't rest. You can call it "the call to destiny" or whatever you like, but if you've ever taken a chance on something that scared the hell out of you because you knew you had to do it, then you know what this is.

I decided to do it. I had fear every day. I set the departure date. Three months from now. I was going to do it. I realized in my moment of decision what courage really is: taking a leap of faith without confidence, embracing your doubt, and jumping in anyway.

As Forrest Gump said, *"My momma told me, 'Life was like a box of chocolates. You never know what you're gonna get.'"*

There are no guarantees in this life. If you're waiting for a guarantee before you take that leap, you'll be waiting until the end of your life. Seize your doubt and jump in if you feel it's right.

The next day, my father showed up with an itinerary and a plane ticket. He handed it to me and said: "This is your ticket to a new life. Now go make it."

I hadn't asked for the ticket. It was a gift. Three months later, full of doubt and uncertainty, I boarded a plane to an unknown destination with no guarantees, and $500 in my pocket. I had a carry-on with a pair of jeans and socks. What it came down to was this: I had two types of fear.

One was the fear of going and not knowing what I was getting into, afraid that things wouldn't work out or I would get homesick.

The other was the fear of staying in a small town and never seeing the world, never knowing what's out there, and never knowing how far I could possibly go. It was the fear of not being an explorer but just sitting around in a bar on a barstool all day talking about all the things I was going to do "someday."

I wonder at times where I'd be if I fear #2 had not been stronger than fear #1. Again, it wasn't about making the right choice, but stepping out of the zone, embracing that fear and taking a chance on something that I really wanted.

When you have no choice, it's the only choice.

I made it to the other side and never looked back. My fear-center had expanded, and I was doing things I had never dreamed possible. Years later, I moved to Japan and explored the depths of Asia. I traveled and had adventures. What had been a fear of not knowing what's out there became a passion for discovery.

Why am I telling you this story? Because there are two sides to the journey. Two people, actually. You're living a double life. There's the person you are, and the person you could be. Maybe self-doubt is holding you back. You're worried about something bad happening. Well, remember that years from now, we will look back on our lives and ask, "Did I do everything I could have done to make the best life possible? Did my fear stop me from living a bold and daring adventure?"

Lesson to learn: There are no negative outcomes. Guarantees are for cars and appliances. There are no guarantees you'll make it if you leap, but if you don't take the chance or the risk, you'll be guaranteed to stay where you are.

I lived in a "stuck zone" for many years. Fear of the unknown made sure I stayed there. Facing your uncertainty and saying, "Well, here goes," guarantees your success—regardless of what happens.

People get stuck when they doubt their chances of success. They weigh all the options, the good and the bad, and ask others for advice about what to do. Something that a mentor once told me is this:

"Fear is always with you. It isn't about becoming fearless and then taking action. You become fearless by taking action, or at the very least, you fear everything much less after you take the initiative."

I look at confidence-building like this: It's a massive puzzle that takes a long time to build; you just have to keep putting the pieces together. You have to start *somewhere* with *something.* It doesn't matter if it's a mini goal of cleaning out an old closet.

Confidence is the other side of living in fear. People who exist in a permanent state of fear are holding themselves back from doing. They think that they're going to lose out somehow. They doubt all ability to succeed.

You can build your confidence up by getting busy. An earlier mentor of mine once said, "You're held back by the mind that's between your own ears. Nobody is taking over your mind except you. Own it and you're free."

Kill your doubt before it kills your dreams. If there's something you're dying to do with your life, and you're being held back, remember that you're not going to live forever. Make the most of the day. It's a better alternative than regretting the things you never did.

"When we really face the fact that we will die one day, we won't embarrass ourselves doing ridiculous things, keeping up the delusion that we're going to live forever. Contemplating our mortality helps us to focus our energy into the practice of transforming and healing ourselves and our world."

— Thich Nhat Hanh

10

RELEASING YOUR FEAR WITH MINDFULNESS

"You are the sky. Everything else is just the weather."

—Pema Chödrön,
author of *When Everything Falls Apart*

Mindfulness is the magic state of getting in touch with your deepest emotions, which are capable of inspiring massive change. You're probably not aware of it, but you practice mindfulness every day in subtle ways.

When you stop to observe a beautiful sunset, or you see something of such beauty that it brings you to tears, or you become aware of another person's pain, and you try to reach out and help, you're moving into your power-centric mindset and connecting with your deeper self through mindfulness.

Mindfulness is your mind existing in the present moment. When you're focused on the now, you're not worrying about the future or regretting the past. You're here in your present moment. With mindfulness, you're reducing your thoughts to simple concepts and in the moment tasks. Life becomes less complicated when you focus on this moment and simple activities such as breathing.

When I found myself focusing on the future in a negative way, such as fearing what could happen, I breathed in deeply several times. If I went back to the past and latched onto a painful memory that caused feelings of regret, I would acknowledge that memory as having already finished and bring my mind back to the present moment.

When we move from the present to the past or the future, we're inviting the possibility of suffering. In our past memories, we suffer regret for those things we can no longer have or that we never obtained; in our future projections, we suffer worry about what we may never get or anticipation that could turn to disappointment.

Breathing is a powerful tool used in mindfulness. When we can focus on our breathing in times of anxiety or worrisome thoughts, we calm down and are drawn into the silence of the world.

Our minds are like rapid express trains. One minute, they're in the past, trying to dig up old memories that are dormant; the next minute, they're in the future, predicting events that will most likely never happen.

When the mind resides in either the past or the future, we're moving into the fear-based mindset. We cannot have power or control in these places. We can only have them in the present.

There's nothing that exists in the past or the future. Yet, we're in a constant struggle with ourselves to stay focused in the now; fear is the action of becoming unfocused. Fear is scattering our thoughts to the wind and hoping they come back with gold. They never do.

Mindfulness implies that you're in control of your mind

at all times. When you're aware of your thoughts as they're occurring and can lead them to concentrate on what you desire, everything else slips away. Focusing on your breathing is such a simple concept that most people overlook it.

You might be uncomfortable meditating and believe that complaining or talking about your problems with someone else is the way to go. While discussing our problems and situations with another is powerful, you have to be careful to whom you talk about your problems. For instance, if you're used to always confiding in your best friend, but he or she is speaking to you from a place of fear, you're going to feel more fearful after having a discussion.

The cycle of fear will repeat itself and you will have accomplished nothing. But talk to someone who is nonjudgmental and has some solid wisdom and you'll walk away feeling more centered. Remember, fear breeds fear. Mindfulness thinking supports a positive mindset.

Self-doubt can always be found in a fearful mind. It comes when you're lurking in the shadows of the past, telling yourself, "If only I had…" Or, when you're straining to look at the distant future, saying, "If only I could…"

Both timeframes are putting your fearful mind on high alert. You feel tense, anxious, and frightened. Happiness, fulfillment, and a sense of purpose can only be found in what you're doing in the present moment. Your past failures—and even your past successes—have no merit anymore.

Be mindful of your present moment. What habits are you building in the now? What words of power are you using to communicate right now? How are you thinking about things? Are you spending your time right now doing something you love? Are you focusing on a goal that's giving you happiness right now?

Being mindful is building awareness into every action, every task, no matter how minute, so that we can stay centered and focused.

Working on your passion is a form of mindfulness. Right now, for instance, I'm writing this book. I could be thinking about writing it, but I'm not; it's happening right now, and then, in the future, you will experience these words days or months from now.

What I am doing now is going to have an impact on the future because I'm creating something to share with people, but I am enjoying it in the present. If readers like what they read here, they might share it with their friends.

For me, doing the work now and not thinking of doing it someday reduces my fear of failure. If I'm working on my passion today, how can I fail?

If I'm wasting my day watching reruns on television, I have a lot to be fearful of because I just lost 4-6 hours of my life that I can never get back. When you spend your time avoiding fearful activities, you invite fearfulness into your life. It permeates your mind, and you age quickly.

Mindfulness is a powerful way of living. It isn't just a technique that you put into practice when you feel like it; mindfulness is a pathway to developing excellence in everything you do. If you practice being in the present moment, your fear-based mindset and obsession with past and future events will become a thing of the past.

This is the path of self-mastery: staying where you are and doing what matters, while watching others race around, trying to figure out what happened in the past, or what they're going to do next. When the world's in chaos, you'll be at peace with yourself.

You don't need years of therapy, and you don't have to wait until things get better. This is another lie that you tell yourself: "The fear will be gone when my life is perfect." It will never be perfect. It never has been. You might experience perfect moments, but you'll never have a perfect life.

That striving for perfection is another way the mind has convinced you that your fear can be controlled at some point in the future when everything works out. You can only have that moment right now.

If you stop your negative thinking and see the perfection in this moment, that's all there is. Your happiness isn't a someday thing; it's a right now thing. It's happening in the now.

Here's how we lie to ourselves about having a perfect life:

- I'll be happy when I finally have enough money.
- I'll be happy when I get the perfect job.
- I'll be happy when I finally get that loan paid off.
- I'll be happy when I have that vacation.
- I'll be happy when I find that perfect partner.

When you're pulled into the events of the future, mindfulness loses its power. You're now living in a state of war with your mind. This is a never-ending loop that's supported by the belief that you're going to be happy in "someday" but not today. Until that day arrives, you'll be stuck in a fearful mind.

A fearful mind is a mind that suffers. Look at all the fearful people around you. Do they look content and happy? Are they living their dreams? Chances are they've cultivated a fearful mind, and to escape it, they're latching onto a time in the future when they'll be less fearful.

Start to practice your mindfulness way of living today. Make it a way of life and not just something you do sparingly when you have time. You'll cultivate a deeper level of thinking focusing on the actions today that are building a better tomorrow. The past is important but serves as a reminder of how far you've come; there's nothing to do in the past anymore.

The future is built on what you're doing today. If you want to predict your future, look at what you're doing right now. As we discussed already, you can stay present by avoiding mindless activities that waste your life.

By moving from mindlessness to mindfulness, your attitude makes a complete shift. Mindfulness promotes higher levels of focus and concentration. You can assess your fear-based thoughts from a peaceful mind more readily than from a mind that is trying to escape.

11

EXPANDING YOUR FEAR-BASED CENTER

"The mind, once stretched by a new idea, never returns to its original dimensions."

— Ralph Waldo Emerson

This is a powerful strategy that's designed to move you from a place of helplessness to one of power. It's a step-by-step process that you can have a lot of fun with because it gets you to do something every day that moves you from comfortable complacency to joyful satisfaction.

It's called the "big-elastic strategy" (or "rubber-band strategy"). You know how a rubber band works? Stretch it those first few times, and it resists. Keep doing it, and eventually, the band expands to cover a larger space.

All of us exist in a level of complacency. We call this our "comfort zone". It's the place where mediocrity promotes fear and encourages us to live below our potential and within certain limitations.

If you stay in your comfort zone and never make any effort to push out of it and explore new possibilities, your skills will get outdated, your thinking will become stagnant, and you will repeat a lot of the same old thought patterns. This will recreate your past, and, as the saying goes, "Do what you've always done, and you'll get what you've always gotten."

You have what it takes right now to start pushing on your comfort zone. Do something that's not comfortable and enjoy it. Take a risk. When I say risk, I mean do something that you would normally say NO to.

A friend of mine had never traveled out of state before. In fact, getting to an airport was a major feat. One day, she decided that the fear she had of staying stuck in one place and never seeing anything else was so great that she bought a ticket for Europe and took a two-week holiday. She could have just flown to another city but decided to just do it and fly to the other side of the world.

There was a lot of fear leading up to this: She had fear when she got a passport, but she did it; she had fear when she went to the travel agency and booked the flight, but she did it.

She said she almost cancelled twice.

She had anxiety when she got to the airport and had to go through security. But she *had* to do it. And then something changed. She told me, "When I got to the airport and all those steps were behind me, I realized… the hard part is over. Now the best part of the trip is ahead of me!"

None of this would have been possible if she had stayed home, just thinking about it.

All these first-time experiences were part of stretching the elastic band and expanding her fear-based center.

I've been through similar experiences many times. But doing it the first time and experiencing that feeling of being uncomfortable was always part of the process and part of the journey.

Do something that you normally wouldn't do and soon, you'll be doing the things that you once thought were impossible to do.

Don't wait until you feel more confident before taking action. Confidence grows *after* you put your foot forward and move in the direction of your dreams.

Don't wait until the time is perfect; it's *never* perfect. The best time to do something is *now.*

As you do more, you grow to handle more. This world is full of so many opportunities for those who act. When you expand your fear-based center and put yourself out there, you're setting yourself up for receiving these opportunities.

It's not just action that expands your fear-based center but your thoughts as well. In fact, you should pay particular attention to your thoughts. Your thoughts control your actions and words. Before you do anything, you'll have a thought about it. As you change your thoughts, you streamline everything else to work together.

We all have thoughts that are caught in an old loop, and worn-out beliefs that don't support our values or goals. Adjusting your thoughts will change the direction of your intentions.

Taking Small Steps in Gentle Strides

You don't have to take big leaps to expand your fear-based center. All change begins with simple steps, and small steps are easier to take than big leaps. There are a lot of things you can do today to start this new habit of expanding your comfort zone or fear-based center.

Start with this: What's something you want to do but you've been putting off because you weren't sure where to begin? Write it down right now.

Here are some examples:

- Signing up for a course
- Creating a website or blog?
- Reaching out to someone who is "above you"
- Starting an exercise program or joining a marathon
- Quitting your job and working for yourself from home

Once you've established what you're afraid of doing, make a note of all the actions you could take to achieve these goals. All these little actions are going to expand your fear-based center.

If you don't feel uncomfortable, it could be that you're still trying to play it safe. If so, push yourself a little further. Do one thing on your list that makes you say, "Wait, what am I, insane?"

I've had many moments like this. What at first seemed like a crazy idea later turned into a great triumph.

Even if it failed.

I've always wanted to play the piano. I've had a piano in my home for years. Never touched it. I would feel overwhelmed if I sat down at it, not knowing what the keys were or unable to read the music.

One day, I asked my seven-year-old daughter to give me a short lesson on learning the notes. I committed to learning one key a day. The next day, I expanded to two keys. Within a month, I was playing a simple song. I still couldn't play the piano with much confidence, but a month before that, I knew nothing about notes or keys. Now, I knew something. I continue to expand on this a little bit every day.

The anxiety I had around this issue has also disappeared along with my ignorance.

Action Task

Plan out your risks one day/week at a time.

At the beginning of each week, I have a one-hour session with myself when I plan my goals for the week. I make an action plan for each day and what I'll work on. Included in this is a list of risks that I plan to take; if it doesn't scare me, I can always adjust it until I feel scared. Getting scared is part of the fun. This is when you know you're planning to expand your fear-based center to new heights of awesomeness.

Have objectives and make a list of the actions you're taking to achieve your objectives. Before you know it, the goals you once believed impossible are now your reality. You've expanded from your comfort zone into a new zone that consists of:

Freedom. Personal Power. Confidence. Mastery.

Now, what action are you taking this week to expand your fear-based center?

12

EMBRACING FEAR ON THE ROAD LESS TRAVELED

"Inaction breeds doubt and fear. Action breeds confidence and courage. If you want to conquer fear, do not sit home and think about it.

Go out and get busy."

— Dale Carnegie

If we're going to take action against the stuff we fear, the first step is to acknowledge that the fear exists. If you do nothing, you get nothing, and nothing changes. You stay stuck in a mediocre state of living. Life is a short journey, and you should do as much with it as you can.

You can live with your fear and leverage it to your advantage, or you can shrink away and hide, resisting all efforts to change and make a difference. You're full of choices. You can choose at any given moment; you can choose your attitude toward any situation and adapt to the circumstances.

Your attitude toward the situation will have one of two outcomes: You'll be either paralyzed by fearful thoughts or empowered to act by positive thoughts. As Dale Carnegie said:

"Inaction breeds doubt and fear."

When you take the lower path and avoid taking action by using resistance tactics, such as distraction or retreat, you only bury your problems deeper.

Deceiving ourselves into believing unresolved issues are taken care of, they never really go away. People who are drawn into procrastination live with a high level of fear. They become overwhelmed with the simplest of tasks, and their fear is really their subconscious trying to communicate with them.

Choosing the path of inaction is choosing a path to suffering. Think about it. That which you resist, persists. What we ignore becomes another task on our mental to-do list that creates an unseen stress pattern. Always unseen but lurking under the surface.

We fail to gain any confidence or courage if we act without purpose.

Sticking with the Difficult Path

I heard some really good advice from a friend of mine once that I've applied for sticking with tough situations: "Everything passes. You can do nothing, and it will pass. You can do something, and time will still pass. But if you do something with delivered attention, you'll utilize that time in the moment and create a tsunami of success for all your future days to come."

Scott Peck, the bestselling author of *The Road Less Traveled*, once said:

> *"Life is difficult. This is a great truth, one of the greatest truths. It is a great truth because once we truly see this truth, we can transcend it. Once we truly know that life is difficult,*

once we truly understand and accept it, then life is no longer difficult. Because once it is accepted, the fact that life is difficult no longer matters."

You must embrace this difficult path if you're going to overcome the obstacles holding you back. The difficulty is the path. The way to freedom is through the toughest days of your life. Unfortunately, this isn't the message that many people are receiving these days.

Life should be fun, yes, and we should be happy and enjoy ourselves. We should share this joy with others. But keep an eye on your challenges and drive yourself to get over those problems holding you back. This is how you can build more confidence into your life and empower yourself to get more done and stay focused in the moment.

People learn to fear life less by doing the things they fear the most. If there were an easier way, I'd give it to you. Don't fall for quick gimmicks or the "fast lane" to success. I've taken these paths before and they all ended the same way: I either lost hope or I was abandoned.

I use a reverse-engineering technique when I need to motivate and empower myself to take action toward something. Instead of visualizing the success of what I hope to achieve (a new book, a website, etc.), I ask myself, "What are the consequences if I don't finish this?"

Where will I be one year from now if I keep doing the same disempowering actions: watching TV when I could be writing, playing on Facebook when I could be setting up my online entrepreneur business, or drinking every weekend when I could be setting up meetings with potential customers?

Ask yourself, "Where will I be if I take action by investing time in all the wrong activities?"

I can tell you the answer. You'll be doing the same things years from now and regretting not doing what you could have done to make all the difference. I know because I wasted years watching TV, playing games, and doing the wrong stuff. That all changed when I made a conscious choice to empower my life further.

I share these lessons with you now, so you can do the same. There's no magic formula or hidden talent involved. It doesn't matter how smart you are (or not!). What people see as "raw talent" is really hard work. It's easy to say, "Take action, and you'll overcome your fear."

As you know by now, it isn't easy and takes daily discipline. But the reward comes after. The good stuff is out there, but you have to start digging for it today.

Robert Frost, an American poet, once said:

> *"I took the road less traveled by,*
> *and that has made all the difference."*

I love that expression, and I use it to empower people to take action toward the things that scare them and do what's difficult—no matter the obstacles that lie in front of them. Just imagine where you'll be in one year, one month, or even next week if you do what's difficult *now*. Think about the difference you'll make, not just in your own life but, in the lives of the people you could help.

The difference is in the amount of effort applied to your life's purpose. Run from what scares you, and you might take the "easy" way out, but it's a trap.

Stand tall, face your difficulties, and work to get through your goals, and you're living the road less travelled. There's no better way to live than doing what you love and doing it well.

How will you live your life on your road less traveled? Try these action tips:

- Open up and observe what you fear.
- Let the fear in. Open the window to your soul and accept your fear as a necessary entity. What's the worst that can happen?
- Think about all the days you've lived in fear of doing the things that you really wanted to do. Has any of the stuff that you thought would be so bad really happened?
- Visualize your life at the end. See yourself as having overcome the obstacles and fears that held you back. See yourself tackling your greatest adversary and winning. Imagine what it will be like when you can look back on your life with a feeling of triumph that your journey was well-lived.
- Don't give up. Right now, start doing the one thing you have always wanted more than anything.
- Embrace your fearful life and thank your fears for giving you the opportunity to grow.

13

LEVERAGING FEAR FOR GREATER EMPOWERMENT

"You gain strength, courage and confidence by every experience in which you really stop to look fear in the face. You are able to say to yourself, 'I have lived through this horror. I can take the next thing that comes along.' You must do the thing you think you cannot do."

— Eleanor Roosevelt

As we've seen in this book, our fears are not going away. We can't just eliminate them and expect them to not return. Instead, we can change our attitude toward the fear we have. This is the leverage that you can apply to any fearful situation that comes up.

I mentioned earlier that acknowledging fear exists is extremely empowering. When you can identify with what scares you, it moves you into a strategic position to do something about it. Your willingness to take action and do something is the first step.

Now let's take a look at the common fears people have and what you can to do manage them. This is a form of eliminating your fears so you can move forward. Just remember that you'll always experience fear when you're challenged.

Make it a goal to challenge yourself as much as you can. Do the things that others won't do. Say YES when you would normally say NO. Say YES when others say NO. Do something that moves you forward instead of hiding or feeding into a distraction to stay stuck.

Most people are afraid of dying or getting sick. Well, you're going to die and get sick someday; that is a reality. But, while this is a natural fear for everyone, you can still leverage this to your advantage.

It comes down to choosing your attitude about the situation. Will you let this fear of getting sick cause you to worry? What could you do to reduce this fear?

First of all, you can acknowledge that you have the fear. Second, you have a choice here: A) continue to be afraid, or B) do something about it. Most people will choose step B because living with fear is painful if it's all you have to focus on.

Now what would be the opposite of being in fear of getting sick? You could start exercising. Eat better food. Make your body as healthy as it can be. Do this, and you'll be too focused on feeling good to fear sickness and death. You're still going to die someday, but you could extend your life by putting in more cardio reps every day.

We become overwhelmed with our fears when we don't know what to do. We blame ourselves for being cowards or labeling ourselves as "weak" if we lack the know-how or intelligence to figure it all out. The internal voices also give convincing evidence that we're nothing but failures, lacking the common sense and wisdom to sort things out.

Leveraging your fear by applying simple strategies is the

edge we need to overcome tough obstacles. What happens is, the fear that's holding you back is the same paradigm that can help you out of a bad spot.

Here are the examples of fears and the action leverage you can apply to overcome anything that's keeping you stuck.

1. Fear of Poverty: For years, I was afraid of living in poverty. I worried about money all the time. I decided that this was turning into serious anxiety. I decided to do something about it by setting up my account so that 20% of the salary was funneled away into another account.

Making the habit automatic made me feel 10 times better about my financial situation. The leverage is saving money automatically. In 10 years, you'll have a good-sized nest egg. If you do nothing, in 10 years, you'll still have nothing no matter how much you think about it.

Action Leverage: Set up your account so that you're automatically paying 10% to yourself with each paycheck. We're stressed out about finances because we haven't set up our system to deal with this. Check out David Allen's book *The Automatic Millionaire* to see how this is done.

2. Fear of Rejection: The fear of rejection is a major obstacle that stops us from asking for things we want, taking advantage of opportunities, and stretching out of our comfort zones. Rejection is a universal issue that most people deal with to varying degrees.

In severe cases, it's extremely paralyzing. But rejection can be overcome. You can overcome your fear of being told NO and learn to love your life by doing more without the fear of being rejected.

Action Leverage: Make a habit of getting rejected. Check out rejection therapy or read my book on rejection called *Rejection Reset.* Purposely get yourself rejected and desensitize yourself to it. Within a couple of weeks, you'll be amazed at how the fear vanishes.

Being rejected is a core emotional pain point for millions of people. They expend tons of energy engaged in activities to avoid rejection. If they went the other way and leveraged opportunity as a chance to be turned down so they could redirect their efforts elsewhere, it would change their entire outlook.

3. Fear of Loss: This is the fear that breeds scarcity, one of the biggest causes of fear I have encountered. More people act irrationally from this fear than any other. The fear of loss is what deceives people into lying, cheating, manipulating, and stealing.

Living with the fear that we'll be cheated out of what belongs to us, we resort to doing the very actions that we fear happening to us. The fear of loss governs greed. It turns people into Scrooges, and they hold back from giving because they fear living with less.

Action Leverage: Give away what you're afraid of losing. If you're afraid of losing love, give it away. If you're afraid of losing money, give it away. Afraid of losing happiness? Give a happy moment to someone. What you give away is yours to keep. What you hold onto with fear ends up escaping your tight grasp. Give it away and you'll never fear losing it.

4. Fear of Deprivation: For many years, I lived in fear of having less. I wanted so many things, and I would often complain about the things I couldn't have. Then, it occurred to me one day that the solution to this fear was so obvious.

After reading a book by Jack Canfield called *The Aladdin Factor*, I realized that my fear stemmed from a deeper fear of asking for what I desired. Once I realized that and acknowledged the source of the fear, I was able to do something with it. So, I started asking for what I desired.

Action Leverage: Make a list of all the things you've ever desired but were afraid to ask for. Is it more love from someone? Is it more time off? Do you desire someone to fix your flat on your car? Whatever it is you desire, there's someone who can give it to you. Ask and you *will* receive. Don't ask and you'll be sure to not get it.

Make a list of your fears. Write everything down; record it in your phone if you want to. But make note of what you fear. Acknowledge that the fear exists. Then, come up with your action leverage plan.

What will you do to cancel out this fear? There's a solution for every fear. You can implement your leverage action plan toward anything and have amazing results in days.

By applying leverage strategies, you're getting yourself out of a rut and pushing past your comfort zone or fear-based center. By doing something instead of just sitting back and accepting things as they are, you're pushing yourself to break out of your limitations.

This isn't just progress; it's empowerment.

You're empowering your fear to do the things you're afraid to do...and you're doing them anyway. By asking yourself and acknowledging what you're afraid of, you can create action tasks to push through it.

- Do you fear poverty? You can save more money by setting up an automatic saving system. You can give more away to people who need it. You can focus on thoughts of gratitude, instead of thoughts of "getting".

- Do you fear being alone? You can get involved in a group of some sorts and make friends. You can get counseling or talk to someone about your fear because it may be a deeper psychological issue.
- Do you fear rejection? You can try getting rejected. Make a game out of it.
- Do you fear failure? Think of a time in your life when you failed. Did you survive it? Are you still here?

You can see how this works. In the previous chapter, we looked at the ways people resist fear and change. Your instinct is to run, but this empowers your fears to react stronger.

When you stand up to fear with deeper conviction and stop running, you become naturally confident. Self-esteem is boosted. Faith in yourself is restored.

We become overrun with our fears because they often seem or appear bigger than we are. We're deceived into believing that we can't handle what's happening or that there's no way out of this.

The inner voices start to chatter up, and we tune into their bullshit, making them the authority in our lives. When we tune into the inner voices, we tune everything else out, including common sense and reasoning.

We base our current chances of success on past outcomes.

- I'll always get rejected because…
- I'll always fail because I always have…
- I'll never find anyone who likes me, and I'll spend the rest of my life alone because…
- I won't succeed because…

The excuse train is never-ending. You can turn these lies around and leverage action to dismantle any power they have. When you do this, the game changes. But don't just take my word for it.

Only you can take the initiative and implement your own strategy.

Start to identify with your fears. Target the fears that are holding you back from moving forward. Identify your most powerful fear today and come up with just 5-10 steps you can take to counterattack. This takes practice but soon it will become a powerful habit.

Make it a personal challenge to do the things you are afraid to do. Do what scares you, and you'll develop a level of confidence and self-assurance that you've never had before.

"If you look into your own heart, and you find nothing wrong there, what is there to worry about? What is there to fear?"

— Confucius

14

TRUSTING IN THE JOURNEY: THE FINAL TRUTH

"I have a suit in my closet with the pocket cut out. It's a reminder to me that I won't be taking anything with me. The last one I wear won't need any pockets."

— Dr. Wayne W. Dyer

Let me share the last truth in this book.

You're going to die someday.

That might be thirty years in the future, or it could be tomorrow. But the fact is, you're living in a heavenly body that's destined to get old, sick, and die.

When you can fully accept this, there isn't much else to fear.

You have nothing to hold onto and no fear of losing anything. You no longer have to worry about your bills; there are no deadlines, and nobody to feel angry at.

You're dying, and when you leave this place, all the stuff you've spent a lifetime accumulating, learning, and loving is staying behind: all your belongings and memories; the cash in your pocket; and the last air in your lungs. Your attachments and grievances, fears and regrets—everything goes. You can finally release it all.

You take nothing with you.

Your possessions will go to someone else.

Your job will go to someone else.

Your house, your car, and all the things you collected will go to someone else.

Your thoughts, fears, and knowledge will no longer matter. Those who loved you will hold onto what remains, and you're free to leave this place.

You own nothing and you will have nothing except what you take with you.

So really, what are we afraid of doing with our lives? Will holding onto fear make the journey any easier?

When your life is stripped down to the bare essence of what it really means to live your life, there's an intense feeling of complete vulnerability. When you look up at the moon and the stars at night and you ponder that they've been there for billions of years, and that beyond all that space are millions of other galaxies perhaps similar to this one, your problems shrink down to an insignificant size.

You can see your world as a small piece of a smaller whole.

So, I ask you again: *What are you afraid of?*

I believe that many people are afraid they will die and never have anything good to speak of their lives. They've spent years chasing job positions, paychecks, and working hard to pay for stuff they didn't need in the first place. Now what? In the end, what does it matter?

We're asking ourselves critical life-changing questions: What good did I do? What difference did I make? Are there no second chances? Will I be remembered? How will I be remembered?

I knew a man once who was diagnosed with terminal cancer. His two children also hated him. He admitted he wasn't a very good father and that he hadn't spoken to them in years. But when he found out that he was terminally ill, he wrote a letter to each of them telling them how much he loved them and how he wished he had been a better father. He was able to pass away knowing that, at least, he had done something in those final days instead of leaving those negative feelings behind.

We see celebrities, presidents, and people of great wealth and fame leave this earth every day. They're leaving behind legacies that a few will follow, until eventually they're forgotten as well.

Time has its way of eroding all things.

Many of us live each day as if it's just another day. We don't think about our death unless faced with a terminal illness diagnosed beforehand or facing a dangerous situation. When you see life as a temporary gift and not something to be wasted, you connect on a deeper level with your human side.

You value the love in a relationship. You value your time on a day off and do as much as you can. You value the work you do. You value the people in your life, and all the little things that drove you crazy. You value your memories—the good and the challenging.

Look to the stars and think about all that's out there. Look inside yourself and see all that's in there. Push your attachments to the back of your mind. They're illusions that have no control over you unless you give them permission.

Attachments to things aren't real. Everything you have, no matter how much you have, eventually belongs to somebody else. When you "buy to own," you're only renting for a short time.

Put aside your fears of getting sick. Why worry about it if you know you're going to die. You are. You will get sick. Your body, a vessel for your soul while you're here, no matter how strong it is, will one day deteriorate and give out.

The best you can do for yourself is to take care of what you have. You fear getting ill? Eat more healthy foods. Exercise. Breathe in deeply 10 times a day. Keep your stress levels low. Focus on your positive thoughts. All these things you take for granted can extend your life and, better yet, add quality to your lifestyle.

Create thoughts of gratitude, not for how much you have acquired in your life, but for how much you had the chance to give away.

So, give away everything you can.

Expect nothing back in return.

If something does come back, give that away too.

Let go of the suffering you've been holding onto.

Just release it.

Steve Jobs once said:

> *"We don't get a chance to do that many things, and everyone should be really excellent. Because this is our life. Life is brief, and then you die, you know? And we've all chosen to do this with our lives. So, it better be damn good. It better be worth it."*

So, the questions to ask yourself are:

- What are you going to do with your life from now on?
- Will you live differently from today?
- Will you fill your days with joy or continue to worry, fear, and experience anxiety?
- Are you ready to choose your life and not have it chosen for you?
- Are you going to live out the rest of your days knowing

that you can be a person who matters?

Mediocrity doesn't exist in death. It doesn't have to exist while you're living, either.

Thich Nhat Hanh said:

> *"We need to free ourselves from these ideas that we are just our bodies, when we die. When we understand that we are more than our physical bodies, that we didn't come from nothingness and will not disappear into nothingness, we are liberated from fear."*

You can do it. You're free to choose, you're free to be, and you belong to nothing and nobody.

Embrace your life.

Live it as if you have no more lives left to live.

Live it once and do everything you have ever dreamed of doing without fear or regret.

Conclusion

MASTER YOUR FEAR

"Fear comes from uncertainty. When we are absolutely certain, whether of our worth or worthlessness, we are almost impervious to fear."

— William Congreve

We've come to the end of the book. Before we part ways, there are just a few final thoughts I'll leave you with. In my brief time on this planet, I've come to learn several things about managing fear that I'll share with you.

We're all afraid. It's just a part of our humanness. But it doesn't have to disempower you. You can take charge by saying NO to the fear.

You will always have fear. I've read a lot of books on this topic, and some people claim that you can get rid of fear. I don't know about that, but I do know that fear is like any other emotion. It can be mastered if you don't ignore it.

Acknowledge that you're afraid, and then, using the techniques we covered in this book, you can leverage your fear to control your situation.

Everyone has multiple fears about different parts of their

lives. Some people are afraid of getting sick, and someone else fears going bankrupt. You might have anxiety about a presentation you are doing, or a fear of your first date with someone you really like. Whatever it is, the fear is part of the course and you can handle it. You will get through it if you go through it.

The fear is not your master; you are. I know it's easy to feel controlled by the things that scare us, especially when it comes to getting out there and doing them. But that's the best way to get over your fears: by getting out there and doing them, even when it feels overwhelming.

Now, the question is: What are you going to do with what you've learned in this book? Will you simply leave it behind and start reading something else? Or will you reflect on your fear and decide to do something about it?

Remember, you don't have to do everything at once. Take one area of your life you want to challenge and just do something about it. Make an action list, even if your actions are "baby steps." The key is momentum, as we've discussed.

Here are 5 simple reminders:

- Create a relationship with your fear.
- Build confidence in your ability by doing what scares you.
- Keep pushing yourself a little more each day.
- Fail as much as you can. Desensitize yourself to it.
- Embrace your life; live each day as if it were your last.

Give! Give! Give!

People who live in fear of life are missing out on a great deal of gifts they have to offer. When we let fear live our lives for us, it affects everything from social interactions to taking advantage of once-in-a-lifetime opportunities. When our minds are corrupted by fear-based thinking, we hold onto it with the fear of letting go.

Instead of sharing our abundance, love, and wisdom, we struggle to hold onto it for fear of losing it. You can't lose what you don't have, and you can't fully appreciate what you have if you're holding onto it for fear of losing it. It's a double-edged sword. If you want to be free, be willing to give.

We try to maintain and hold onto our power by clinging to the stuff that eventually controls us. For example, we hold onto our money as if it belongs to us. Remember: empty pockets. Everything you "own" or possess is just in your presence for the moment. Eventually, it's going to leave.

People's fears are irrational when they can look at it from a nonjudgmental position. Scarcity thinking removes our ability to share any part of ourselves.

Instead of helping people, we fear reaching out in case they take advantage of us. Instead of giving praise, we deliver criticism; in place of sharing love, we act out in anger. In place of kind words, we deliver words that hurt.

When we view everything from our fear-based mindset, it permeates our personality and injures our quality of character. Like Ebenezer Scrooge, we live to defend what's ours and see others as parasites, intent on taking our belongings. What we protect with our fear ends up owning us. What we defend becomes our enemy.

Fearful people hold onto money, so they don't lose it.

Fearful people withhold love until they get love first. They think, "I'll only give if you do."

Fearful people become emotionally detached from their fellow humans and grow more attached to what they're protecting.

If they do give, it's because they want to get something in return. This isn't giving; it's usury. They're willing to loan what's theirs just as long as they get it back with interest.

When you focus on giving away the stuff that you're afraid of, you're deciding to take back your power. Over the years, the definition of "power" has lost its meaning. We're taught that money is power; control is power; and having a better education, more stuff, and being popular is power. But is it true?

One of my earlier mentors once told me: "Never put your faith or future in anything that has the potential to disappear overnight. Never believe in what isn't yours."

Believing in Big, Magic Moments

If there's anything that I want you to take away from this book, it is this message:

Believe in your dreams, even when life sucks and you feel like giving up. You'll have many days like this, but if you work at reducing your fear by doing the things that scare you the most, you'll one day look back on your life and wonder *what was the big deal anyway?*

I've done many things in my life that I once would have considered impossible. When you're doing the impossible, you're on the right road.

As long as you keep pushing forward, you'll never have to live with the regret of looking back and saying, "If only I had taken the road less traveled."

No, not you. I want you to get to the end of your journey and say, "I'm glad I decided to do that."

Live your big magic each day. This implies to keep moving forward and keep pushing. Don't wait for motivation or that perfect moment. You'll be waiting forever while life is passing you by.

On the days you need to rest and reflect, take that time for yourself. We need to stop, think, assess, and plan our journey as much as we need to walk it.

As Lao Tzu said:

> *"A journey of a thousand miles begins with a single step."*

What step are you taking today? What step will you take tomorrow? If you lack confidence, take a look at the successful people you know who doubted their abilities and chances of success. You can see these people all around you. It doesn't matter who they are.

One of my biggest heroes was Bruce Lee. He came from a poor background and faced a lot of adversity to get to where he wanted to be.

Bruce Lee said:

> *"Life is hard for a reason; because we're designed to value hard work and effort. Nothing we've ever valued came for free. With difficulty comes character, strength, humility, and perseverance. If you wish to have more of it, wish for more of it."*

Persevere in your efforts. Know exactly what you want. Then, identify the fears that prevent you from taking action when you feel resistance holding you back.

- Is it a phone call that you're afraid of making?
- Is it a relationship that has to end before you can move on?

- Is it your internal critic, feeding you lies about your self-worth?
- Is it a technical issue, such as using a piece of software?

Nothing is easy, but it isn't impossible either. Everything seems difficult until you jump in and start doing it.

Your big, magic moment is when you see the results of your efforts. But it's not just about the outcome. It's the small steps along the way. That one tough spot that you had to circumnavigate around before you could go to the next stage. There are lots of those. Each one is a mini challenge in itself, but that's how you get from here to there.

That's how you work with your fear instead of letting it keep you stuck. That's the definition of success.

As Susan Jeffers, the bestselling author of *Feel the Fear and Do It Anyway,* said:

> *"Each time you can see the gift in life's obstacles, you can handle difficult situations in a rewarding way. Each time you have the opportunity to stretch your capacity to handle the world, the more powerful you become."*

Push yourself to do just one thing today that expands your fear-based center. Let your resistance in. Feel it when it jumps in your way.

Let the self-doubt in, as well. Acknowledge its presence. Be aware of the language you're using to empower your self-doubt. Do you agree with what your mind is saying?

The only one in control of this is you. You're choosing your thoughts. Nobody else is in charge. This is extremely empowering when you recognize how much control you really do have. If you feel helpless or weak, it has very little to do with external forces.

Remember, Viktor Franklyn was Surrounded by the harshest conditions on earth and death close by every moment of his existence; even then he realized that he had a choice.

We all have the same two choices.

Make your choice.

Do it or not.

Live your life or not.

You can choose to create big magic in your life or settle for little whispers of what could have been.

I hope that you've gained some valuable insight into tackling your fear and that you're ready to put this into action.

I wish you the best of success, and I'll see you again soon… either here or there.

Scott Allan

https://scottallanauthor.com/

"The cave you fear to enter holds the treasure you seek."

— Joseph Campbell

DEVELOP THE HABIT OF INTENTIONAL THINKING

If you work on any habit, make the first one a habit to control your thoughts. This is one of the best habits you will ever develop—more so than time management or even eating habits.

Once you have the habit of feeding your thoughts the information you want them to have, the rest just falls into place. Consider your thinking as the central core to all else that is happening.

Thinking creates emotions. It creates responses and is responsible for the kingdom of your mind. People who thrive in a successful environment have arrived there because they have powerful thoughts that guide them every step of the way.

How many successful negative thinkers do you know? I don't know too many, but I know a lot of positive thinkers who work hard and believe that what they are doing is making a difference.

A person who has a positive mental attitude also has a pattern of strong positive thoughts. I know there are tons of books and material out there on why we need to maintain a positive attitude throughout life. The reasons are obvious. Negative thoughts are dangerous—just as dangerous as smoking or drinking heavily. In a way, negative thinking is also an addiction.

People fall into the pattern of reacting to a situation from a negative point of view and this becomes their default mindset. When you live this way, you'll attract like/negative people to engage with. Positive people who are upbeat and happy have no reason or interest to share time with people who bring them down.

Negative people are the same way. If they can't convert positive-minded people to join in their misery, they find someone who will listen. Like attracts like. You can have one side or the other but not both.

If your default habit is reacting negatively, that is okay. You can change this. It won't happen overnight, but if you maintain persistent focus and remember to force the habit to change, you will change it. Negative behavior is addictive and easy to fall into. Positive behavior is addictive, as well, but more difficult to maintain because of the work you have put in.

There are no advantages to having an NMA. You might be thinking "I already know that," but regardless, I see many people every day who have a big chip on their shoulder and they are looking for someone to unload all their misery on. There are also some people who think they are positive players, but in fact it is an illusion.

If you are unhappy, discontent, dissatisfied, live in fear, believe in limitations, or have a lot of anger and you don't know why, chances are you suffer from some form of a negative mental mindset. And if you do, that is okay. That is why we are here.

I believe too many people are slaves to their own vices. They think they have no choice in so many situations. However, it is just the opposite. It is not the situations we have to learn to adapt to; it is the power of our mind, and how it is trained to perceive its surroundings. You cannot control others (and you shouldn't), and if they try to control you, that is their choice. *They* will suffer for it.

Failing to develop your positive mindset is setting yourself up for failing in most other areas too. If you fall into the bad habit of not working on your attitude, you risk falling into a negative mindset. Remember this: You have two paths you can take. One path leads to forging strong relationships, quality lifestyle, and turning your thoughts into dreams.

The other path is the opposite and is the path unfortunately most people choose "unconsciously" when they lose touch with themselves. Believing in limitations, using words that demean or harm yourself and others, complaining and bickering, or reacting to your emotions without thinking is the way to suffering.

Do you like suffering? I don't know of anyone who does, and yet every day, people act out in ways that add to the suffering of either themselves or somebody else. The news is rife with it. Our communities are full of it. You can start with your own temple of success in your mind. Make a choice to be different, and you will be. By not making a choice, you choose the other path by default.

Your positive mindset is the foundation on top of what everything else is achieved. You can't build the home of your dreams on a faulty foundation.

Core Strategies for Creating a Positive Attitude

Here are two strategies for building and maintaining a positive attitude that, if practiced, will change the course of your life.

1. **Stay connected with your thoughts.** Observe what is happening with your thinking, and then start to make

slight adjustments. This won't happen instantly. And even for people who are highly positive, creative, and successful, they, too, must stay frosty and be on top of things. A positive mental attitude is not a goal to achieve. It is a state of mind you must work your way into, and then maintain. Just as a garden is never truly rid of its weeds because new ones crop up every day, your mind needs constant attention, too.

2. **Pay attention.** When a negative thought creeps in, just let it happen. You can't combat everything, and you are going to have bad days when the world is shit, and you wonder why you are here at all. It happens. When you have one of those "life is absolute shit" days, let it be. It is also unrealistic to think you can be a loving, positive individual made of unstoppable success every day. You won't be, but if you train yourself to be like this most days, you will fare better in the end. Have your bad day, and then get back to it.

Go back through the book and jot down the ways to create a positive mindset. Gratitude, affirmations, and reading self-help books are just a few ways to reinforce your attitude of growth and to get rid of negative thinking. Just doing a few of the things on the list is going to make a big impact on your quality of life.

Here are additional suggestions for creating a PMA:

- Focus on what you love to do and start doing it.
- Leave your failures outside of your mind. Keep them as reminders and lessons learned but they are not your future.
- Make "Affirmation Repetition" a habit. Have a list of affirmations or quotes you can read at the start of

every day. Check the back of this book for affirmation suggestions.

- Do one act of kindness at least once a day.
- Spend 30 minutes with your thoughts every evening. This means turning off all devices, the TV, and shutting yourself away for 30 minutes. This doesn't mean you have to meditate, but just be one with your thoughts.
- A defeat is not a loss; life is not all a streak of wins. You will stumble and fall. Get back up and try it again. Persistence is a major positive skill that is going to give you a huge PMA if you keep it up.
- Write down one thing you are grateful for every day. Do this as soon as you wake up. It will take 10 seconds. Just one thing. Keep a gratitude list. I started to keep one two years ago. I write down one thing every morning or at night that I am grateful for.
- Don't rely on things for your happiness or fulfillment.
- Nobody can make you feel miserable or sad; that is a choice.
- Avoid making time for people who like to waste yours.
- Believe that freedom is your choice; you can either free your mind or keep it enslaved with negative thoughts and images.

What lessons have you learned? You can add them to this list to remind you of what you can do and to see how far you have come. Now that we have the essential elements to create your attitude, what are you going to do with it?